English studies

A GUIDE FOR LIBRARIANS TO THE
SOURCES AND THEIR ORGANISATION

English studies

A GUIDE FOR LIBRARIANS TO THE
SOURCES AND THEIR ORGANISATION

JAMES THOMPSON
BA FLA
Librarian, University of Reading

CLIVE BINGLEY **b** LONDON

FIRST PUBLISHED 1968 AS 'THE LIBRARIAN AND ENGLISH LITERATURE'
BY THE ASSOCIATION OF ASSISTANT LIBRARIANS

THIS EDITION FIRST PUBLISHED 1971 BY CLIVE BINGLEY LTD
16 PEMBRIDGE ROAD LONDON W11
SET IN 10 ON 13 POINT LINOTYPE TIMES
AND PRINTED IN THE UK BY THE CENTRAL PRESS (ABERDEEN) LTD
COPYRIGHT © JAMES THOMPSON 1971
0 85157 127 1

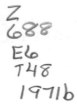

Contents

Introduction

THOUGH THIS BOOK is addressed primarily to librarians, and most especially to students working for the Library Association's part II examinations on the bibliographical organisation of English language and literature, it should also prove useful to many others in the field of English studies.

Only the latter part of the book, which is concerned with the actual administration of an English collection—cataloguing, classification and so on—is entirely professionally orientated. The first, and greater, part is a straightforward survey of the use and contents of the whole range of standard works and sources, and as such can be profitably consulted by anybody with an interest in English studies. And though English literature is the book's main concern, neither American nor Commonwealth literature is neglected in its coverage.

Revision for this second edition has been considerable, but largely bibliographical: incorporating new works (about 30) and new editions (about 65), and rectifying omissions (approximately 50 additional titles have been noted).

The sections on the librarianship of the subject are more or less unchanged, except that in the chapter on cataloguing greater prominence has been given to the new Anglo-American code (for help with which I remain indebted to Mr P K Escreet).

JAMES THOMPSON

MAY 1971

CHAPTER I

An English collection

THE VERY PHRASE 'an English collection' has a vague, comfortable sound to it. It evokes a picture of a haphazard assortment of volumes variously and untidily acquired, and subject to no standards of use or selection other than distinctly personal ones. It is the proper function of a librarian, however, to establish his custody of such a collection on a systematic basis.

His first concern must be the actual literary texts in the collection. Obviously every major author must be represented, and if the librarian can afford only one edition of each, it must be the most appropriate to his library's need. Since the financial state of most libraries protects the librarian from what Arundell Esdaile called 'the unintelligent ambition of a mechanical completeness', the essence of good librarianship lies in skill and judgment in such selection.

The ability to select appropriately is not some kind of magic. It can be achieved by experience and knowledge, but it is also within the capabilities of a student librarian. There exist sufficient bibliographical aids to guide the merest novice: selective bibliographies, comprehensive bibliographies, bibliographies of period and form, bibliographies of individual authors. Such bibliographical aids constitute therefore an essential supplement to an English collection, not only for the librarian, but equally for the users of the collection.

Nor is a librarian normally content to offer only editions of authors, since for their study and appreciation further help is required in the way of critical and biographical studies and commentaries; and the very presentation of a range of authors calls in its turn for the provision of literary histories to give a necessary conspectus, both histories whose treatment is general, and those which deal only with a particular form or period. Further, even the most complete range of authors needs to be augmented by anthologies and collections, and anything less than the most complete depends on them. And if the collection so far assembled is considered in

9

terms of its use by readers, another need becomes plain: the provision of reference material. What would an English collection be without an English dictionary? Apart from dictionaries of language, there must be dictionaries of allusions, quotations, phrases and proverbs. There must be encyclopedias and companions. There must be dictionaries of biography.

Provision does not stop with books. Periodicals are vital in the scientific field, but their importance in the study of literature has a very much longer history. The provision of periodicals, in its train, obliges the librarian of a collection to offer adequate guides and indexes to them. Besides periodicals, an English collection may also contain microforms, manuscripts and theses.

All that has been reviewed up to this point may be regarded as the bibliography of the subject. Selection has been mentioned as the first, and key, function of librarianship in this or any other field. Selection, of course, is not founded only on consulting bibliographies. It involves many other things: the critical use of book reviews, a knowledge of publishers and the book-trade generally, and an awareness of the needs of the collection for which the selecting is being done.

Having selected and successfully obtained (also part of selection) the materials for his English collection, the librarian's next duty is to make an accurate record of them, that is, to catalogue them. There is one infallible way of assessing any library: examine its catalogue. If the building is magnificent, the stock impressive and the staff courteous, all count for nothing if the catalogue is slovenly and patently inaccurate. The cataloguing of an English collection does not present any peculiar difficulties, but standards, as in any cataloguing, must be impeccable.

Classification of books in the field of literature tends to be straightforward, so straightforward that the need for it is often underestimated. But an English collection, like any other collection, is unusable unless it is arranged on the shelves in a definite, consistent way. True enough, once a classification scheme appropriate to the character and use of a particular collection has been found or devised, actual application of the scheme normally presents very few difficulties.

Finally, having selected, catalogued and classified his collection, the librarian must exploit it. Plainly, the provision of a catalogue and a helpful arrangement on the shelves are themselves forms of exploitation, but they must be augmented further: for instance, in a public library, by displays and reading-lists.

A librarian's duty to the collection of which he is custodian does not end with knowledge of his own collection. Bearing in mind the interests of his users, it is also part of his function to know of the existence of other collections, in particular, of outstanding ones. He must also be familiar with current schemes for interlending, specialization, and co-operative acquisition; and acquainted with the work and publications of important societies and associations in the field.

In brief, there is nothing vague or indeterminate either about the contents of an English studies collection nor about the functions of its librarian. The intention of this book is to deal systematically with both.

CHAPTER II

Selective bibliographies

A LIBRARIAN'S USE of bibliographies is of two main kinds. One is when his aim is to establish the existence of a book or article, and here he needs to consult the most complete record, that is, a comprehensive bibliography. The other is when he is seeking guidance on which is the most suitable for a particular purpose of a number of possible books and articles, and in this case he refers to a selective bibliography. It is pointless to argue which, selective or comprehensive, is the more important to him, for both are necessary. But it would be true to say that it is the selective bibliographies which he tends to keep near, if not actually on, his own desk. Most of the stock of an English collection can be chosen on the basis of a careful use of selective bibliographies. They assist the librarian not only in deciding which authors to feature in the collection, but also in deciding in which editions to represent them. More than that, they draw his attention to the whole range of related secondary material: studies, histories, anthologies, reference works.

The best, and most familiar, of the selective bibliographies is *The concise Cambridge bibiliography of English literature, 1600-1950*, edited by George Watson (Cambridge, Cambridge UP, 2nd ed, 1965), and obviously its authority derives from the parent work, of which it is 'a compression by rigorous selection'. Part of the compression results in it restricting its field to 'writers in English native to or mainly resident in the British Isles', and therefore it excludes American and Commonweath authors. Even so, its coverage extends to about four hundred writers, comprising all those ranked as major by the parent work plus a number of minor ones. Arrangement is by period: after a general section, there follow separate sections for the Old English period (600-1100), the Middle English (1100-1500), the Renaissance to the Restoration (1500-1660), the Restoration to the Romantics (1660-1800), the nineteenth century (1800-1900), and finally, the twentieth century (to 1950). Within each period, after an introductory list of period bibliographies, histories and anthologies, authors are arranged in a straightforward alphabetical sequence. Under each author, the treatment is basically the standard ' works by ' followed by ' works about '; specifically, the information given is (i) name (with dates), (ii) bibliographies, concordances, (iii) the main works in order of publication, listing ' only the most *significant* early editions, namely the first edition and that representing the author's final intention ', (iv) collected works, letters and journals, (v) standard works and critical studies. The index includes the names of editors and critics as well as those of the authors treated. *The concise Cambridge bibliography of English literature* is not annotated in any way: the fact that an edition or study is cited indicates that it is an important one. If the librarian or student were restricted to having but one selective bibliography, this would almost certainly have to be it.

The editor of the *Cambridge bibliography of English literature* itself, F W Bateson, has published a selective bibliography of his own, called *A guide to English literature* (London, Longmans, 2nd ed, 1967). He describes it as ' a new kind of literary history ', combining reading-lists and inter-chapters. His first chapter deals with general works on English literature: bibliographies and reading lists, literary histories, anthologies and works of reference. Chapters 2 (Medieval literature), 4 (Renaissance literature), 6 (Augustan literature) and 8 (Romanticism) are ' interpretative inter-chapters ', each followed by a reading-list chapter, the final reading-list covering 1800-1960. The last chapters, chapters 10 and 11, both bibliographical, are on ' Literary criticism in English ' and ' Literary scholarship: an introduction to research in English literature '. Within each of the period divisions, authors are arranged by date of birth, for Bateson is at pains to stress how important a chronological sense is to the student of literature. The value of *A guide to English literature* lies more in the authority and erudition of Bateson than in its approach or arrangement. It is to be respected by the very fact that its compiler can claim to have ' actually used at one time or another the great majority of the books and editions here listed ', and can be relied on to have achieved his intention ' to cover everything of literary or critical importance down to the end of 1966 '. His method of presenting bibliographical information is not by listing, nor even by annotation, but more by narration. He makes authori-

13

tative judgments, applying to various editions and studies words such as ' erroneous ', ' verbose ', ' uncritical ', ' unreliable ', ' woolly '.

Another work in the same style, but nowhere near so pontifical, is Arundell Esdaile's *The sources of English literature: a guide for students* (Cambridge, Cambridge UP, 1928), given as the Sandars Lectures in 1926. Its great virtues are its readability and its gusto. To write a readable book on bibliography is difficult enough: to have been able to produce a series of fascinating lectures on the subject is an awesome achievement. Esdaile's book is a stylish, connected and eloquent treatment of general bibliographies; general catalogues; booksellers' and collectors' guides; book-trade lists of current books; works on different periods, localities, forms and authors; dictionaries of anonyma and pseudonyma; catalogues of private libraries; indexes of book-sales; and private libraries. It must be noted, however, that Esdaile has dated and is now of limited practical use.

There are three notable American contributions to the number of selective bibliographies of English literature. That with the longest history is Donald F Bond's *A reference guide to English studies* (Chicago, Chicago UP, 1962), which is based on Tom Peete Cross's *Bibliographical guide to English studies,* first published in 1919 and in its tenth edition when Professor Cross died in 1951. Cross's original emphasis on ' general sources of information ', that is, on ' the universal bibliographies, the bibliographies of bibliographies, the indexes and classified lists of books and articles, and the bibliographies of dissertations ', has been maintained by Bond, who restates the work's preoccupation with ' the essential sources ', and adds that ' every effort has been made to restrict the material to the indispensable references in each field '. The result is a short, serious ' introduction to the methods and materials of graduate study in English ', which has made the name of Tom Peete Cross perhaps the best-known in the field of selective English bibliography. The items listed are numbered, the last one being 1,230, and are arranged in nineteen sections: descriptive bibliography and typography; treatises on methods of research; bibliographies of bibliographies; universal bibliographies; library catalogues and guides; indexes and lists of newspapers and periodicals; periodical publications containing reviews and bibliographies; learned societies; dissertations; encyclopedias, literary handbooks and lists of reference works; literature, exclusive of literature in America; language; comparative literature; history; biography, genealogy and heraldry; anonymous and pseudonymous literature; auxiliary subjects (for example, auction records, paleography); and American literature. Brief annotations, informative rather than evaluative, are supplied to some items, and the book has two indexes, one of persons, and one of subjects.

Another American guide, shorter and more restrictive still, is Richard D Altick and Andrew Wright's *Selective bibliography for the study of English and American literature* (New York, Macmillan, 3rd ed, 1967). It is concise, bared-to-essentials, with an astringent preface presenting a hard-headed no-nonsense approach: ' we have sought to include only those bibliographies and reference works which are actually used—and usable—by modern scholars '. The two compilers continue in this vein using expressions such as ' common sense ', ' short-winded ', and phrases like ' a well-rounded *vade mecum*,' but they have in fact produced what they aimed to produce: a ' reasonably authoritative guide to research materials ' for the student. It covers bibliographical handbooks, literary encyclopedias and handbooks, literary histories, guides to libraries, bibliographies, dictionaries, periodicals, guides to dissertations, manuscripts and records, and has a section each on history and biography, concluding with a ' Glossary of useful terms ' and an index.

The third notable American contribution, Arthur G Kennedy and Donald B Sand's *A concise bibliography for students of English* (Stanford, California, Stanford UP, 4th ed, 1960), though it describes itself as being ' concise ', is liberal in comparison with Bond and with Altick and Wright. Its numbered items (the last is 5,438) are grouped into fourteen chapters which cover the periods of English literature, prose, poetry, stage and drama, criticism and interpretation, periodicals and series, the English language, folklore and forms of popular literature, literary research, periodical and newspaper bibliographies, printing and the book-trade, library science, general bibliographical guides, and general reference works. Conciseness is achieved in the actual entries, which give only author, title, imprint and pagination, and where there is annotation it is limited to one line or less. There is both an index of authors and a subject index.

A Canadian contribution to the field of selective bibliography of English is supplied by Inglis F Bell and others in *Reference books in English literature: an annotated list of basic books for undergraduates* (Vancouver, Humanities Division of the University of British Columbia Library, rev ed, 1961), which is only thirty-five pages long but is useful in a general way: the minimum list in a handy form. It lists ' with brief annotations, the basic bibliographies, indexes, handbooks, special dictionaries, etc, for students in English literature '.

Quite different from anything described so far, and quite unique, is F Seymour Smith's *An English library* (London, Deutsch, rev ed, 1963), which has as its sub-title 'A bookman's guide ', and which its compiler further categorizes in his introduction as ' a sort of superior bookman's shopping-list at its most modest level, and at its highest . . . a working bibliographical tool supplementing critical histories of English literature '. It began life during the second world war as a forty-page booklet intended as ' a guide to the classics for servicemen and the general public ', and was limited to books in the four great series (Everyman, Collins, Nelson and Worlds Classics), and subsequently developed into a reference work for librarians, booksellers, book-trade students and personal book-buyers. It is concerned now with three categories of books: first, it aims to list ' all the books from *The Canterbury tales,* up to those by writers now dead, of the present century, that by common consent have become classics '; secondly, it gives ' a liberal selection of standard books likely to interest general readers '; and thirdly, it deals with ' minor classics of the past that are reprinted, or in the opinion of the compiler deserve to be '. The important thing to notice is that Smith's guide contains nothing by living writers (with the exception of reference works), and consequently he reminds us that he has also compiled *What shall I read next?* (Cambridge UP for the National Book League) which gives his personal selection of twentieth century books; and though he includes nineteenth century American literary classics, he ignores anything American after the turn of the century. His book is arranged into ten groups: autobiographies and memoirs (including diaries, journals and letters);

biographies (individual and collective); essays, belles lettres and literary criticism (including monographs, collected works and omnibus volumes); fiction (novels and short stories); history (including social and political history, rhetoric and speeches); philosophy and religion (including political and social philosophy); poetry and poetic drama; prose drama; travel, description and topography; and finally, a bookman's reference library. The arrangement within each group or sub-group is rigorously alphabetical by author; each is preceded by a short introductory essay; and all entries are annotated both informatively and evaluatively, Smith using asterisks to indicate his first choices. In all 1,170 authors and about 2,630 books are cited; the 1962 price of each is given; and there is an author index and a title index. The introductory essays are not profound: they are lightweight, chattily informative, and fractionally irritating. But it is, after all, the personal enthusiast to whom they are addressed in spirit no matter what the preface says. However, there is indeed much guidance given, especially for the public librarian, about editions and series. The origins of the book are still obvious: as an example, one may quote from the introductory essay to the fiction section, where Smith refers to ' the level of the fiction produced by Victorian novelists whose books have found permanent places in *Everyman, Worlds Classics* and other series '; plainly, the featuring of a book in a series is a kind of golden seal as far as he is concerned.

Two works which are not concerned only with providing a selective bibliography, but which are nevertheless most useful in that respect, are *Introductions to English literature,* edited by Bonamy Dobrée (London, Cresset Press, 5 vols) and *A guide to English literature,* edited by Boris Ford (London, Cassell, 7 vols: originally, the *Pelican guide to English literature*).

The *Introductions to English literature* are an excellent series of volumes, each dealing with a particular period, each separately written: vol 1, *The beginnings of English literature to Skelton, 1509,* by W L Renwick and H Orton (2nd ed, 1952); vol 2, *The English renaissance, 1510-1688,* by V de S Pinto (3rd ed, 1966); vol 3, *Augustans and Romantics, 1689-1830,* by H V D Dyson and J Butt (3rd ed, 1961); vol 4, *The Victorians and after, 1830-1914,* by E C Batho and Dobrée himself (3rd ed, 1962); and vol 5, *The present age,* by D Daiches (1962). These are scholars of first rank. More

17

than half of each volume is devoted to the bibliography of the subject, and the approach is highly evaluative and practical. The arrangement of the volumes is not uniform; nor are the preliminary comments to their respective bibliographical sections, which vary from, in vol 2, a statement of the aim as being to indicate to the student 'some of the most significant books of the period, the chief editions in which they have been published, and the most important biographical and critical works that can be consulted as helps to the understanding of them', to, in vol 4, the bibliography given being described as 'a list of suggestions which may be supplemented from the biographies of the older writers and from current books of reference'. Despite these varying declarations of intent, the reader or librarian is told in all five volumes which is the best edition of an author's works, which the best life, and which the better critical studies, and everywhere is to be found that invaluable type of evaluation of which the following, under John Arbuthnot, is a prime example: 'Aitken's *Life* has been supplemented, but not displaced, by L M Beattie's more critical *John Arbuthnot, mathematician and satirist* (Harvard and OUP, 1935)'.

Ford's *Guide* is also divided by period: vol I, *The age of Chaucer* (1961); vol II, *The age of Shakespeare* (1961); vol III, *From Donne to Marvell* (1962); vol IV, *From Dryden to Johnson* (1962); vol V, *From Blake to Byron* (1962); vol VI, *From Dickens to Hardy* (1963); and vol VII, *The modern age* (1964). But here each volume is made up of a number of separate essays by experts, for example, in vol IV, V de S Pinto writes on *John Wilmot, Earl of Rochester,* and Ian Watt on *Defoe as novelist.* Rochester and Defoe have been lifetime interests of these two scholars. At the end of each volume there are appended two bibliographical sections, *Appendix for further reading and reference,* and *Authors and works.* The former is subdivided into *The social and intellectual setting* (where are listed histories and works on the social and economic background), and *The literature* (bibliographies, general studies, and studies of particular forms); the latter is alphabetically arranged by author, supplying short chronological biographies and concise bibliographies.

Finally, mention should be made of two selective bibliographies which concentrate on American literature only. The first is Clarence

Gohdes's *Bibliographical guide to the study of the literature of the USA* (Durham, North Carolina, Duke UP, 3rd ed, 1970). Gohdes explains his reasons for compiling this work in his preface: ' In its way, it is comparable to the bibliographical guides to English literature compiled by Arthur G Kennedy, Tom P Cross, and John W Spargo [*A bibliographical manual for students of the language and literature of England and the United States,* not treated in this chapter on selective guides because it is now too much out-of-date]. Their manuals, with varying emphasis and method, contain material on American as well as British literature, but their treatment of the former is relatively incidental and for sound reasons has proved unsatisfactory to Americanists. This book is the first of its kind to see print.' The book has thirty five numbered sections, and within each section this numbering is continued decimally. The arrangement in the sections is deliberately not alphabetically by author in order that Gohdes might be able ' to begin . . . with the most generally used bibliographies or to group titles which have a special affiliation '. The items listed are annotated informatively, and there is both an index of names and an index of subjects. The various sections cover general bibliographies and histories of American literature, particular periods and particular forms, and in addition, materials such as newspapers, periodicals and indexes.

A second selective bibliography of American literature is the *Guide to American literature and its backgrounds since 1890* by Howard Mumford Jones and Richard M Ludwig (Cambridge, Mass, Harvard UP, 3rd ed, 1964). This is more enlightened, and very much less pedestrian, than Gohdes: well-presented, easy to use, and highly informative. The listings are suggestive, say the compilers, not definitive; and the aim is to present in understandable order ' the combination of intellectual and sociological (political) event and literary productivity '. The book is in two main divisions, therefore. The first, dealing with the social and intellectual background, covers general guides, general reference works, general histories, special aspects (for example, education, fine arts), literary history, magazines, and chief historical events 1890-1963. The second division gives fifty one reading lists of major works of American literature, grouped within two main periods: 1890-1919, and 1920-63. The book's method may be illustrated by the following example: in the 1890-1919 period, section 9 is headed 'The West', and there follows a half-page introduction to this topic as a preliminary to a reading list of eleven 'westerns', ranged in alphabetical order of author, from Andy Adams's *The log of a cowboy* to Owen Wister's *The Virginian,* the only detail given for each in addition to author and title being the date of publication. There is an index of authors.

CHAPTER III

Major bibliographies and catalogues

THE THREE FAMOUS NAMES in the history of the bibliography of English literature are Watt, Lowndes and Allibone. Two have about them an unfortunate suggestion of, in Esdaile's phrase, 'the Hope Diamond or the fatal mummy'. Robert Watt, a Glasgow physician, after what he himself described as 'indefatigable labour for nearly twenty years' and 'the sacrifice of a useful life', died without seeing his work published; its printing was delayed by the theft of a portion of the manuscript; the premature death of Watt's son was attributed to the filial assiduity of his bibliographical labours; and, as a consequence of the penury to which Dr Watt's bibliographical endeavours reduced his family, his only surviving daughter died eventually in a Glasgow workhouse. Lowndes fared no better: he died penniless and mentally deranged. Lest would-be compilers of monumental bibliographies be put off entirely, it may be recorded that Allibone remained, according to S J Kunitz and H Haycraft, a 'handsome, gracious-mannered, sweet-spirited, and witty man', and lived to a good age. The really notable thing about these three works is their continuing value: despite the expense, all have been reprinted recently, Watt by Burt Franklin, and Lowndes and Allibone by the Gale Research Company.

Watt's *Bibliotheca britannica* (Edinburgh, 4 vols, 1824) is in two parts. The first part is an alphabetical arrangement of more than forty thousand authors; a short biography is given of each, followed by a chronological list of works in 'their various editions, sizes and prices'. The second part contains the same books arranged by subject. Periodicals and foreign works are covered, and as a whole the work claims to be a combination of encyclopedia, biographical dictionary, a history of early printing, a guide to Greek and Roman classics, and an account of British writers in 'every branch of knowledge and literature'. Its chief value now is for students of eighteenth century literature.

William Thomas Lowndes's *The bibliographer's manual of Eng-*

lish literature (4 vols, 1834, and from 1857 revised by H G Bohn), took Brunet's *Manuel du librairie* as its model. Its sub-title describes it as 'containing an account of rare, curious, and useful books, published in or relating to Great Britain and Ireland'. The arrangement is alphabetical by author, and more than fifty thousand books are noted. For each work there is a concise account of its merits, a description of its 'peculiar *bibliographical* character' (number of copies printed, rarity, dedication, variations in editions), a collation, and the price it brought in sales. Though uneven and often inaccurate, it is still of use.

Samuel Austin Allibone's *A critical dictionary of English literature and British and American authors, living and deceased, from the earliest accounts to the latter half of the nineteenth century* (London, Trübner, 3 vols, 1859-71) contains articles on over forty six thousand authors. Its aim was to direct its users to 'the best works of the best authors', indicating which were the desirable works for school, library and parlour table; in addition, 'a profound deference to the principles of the Christian religion, and a settled disapprobation of the impieties and absurdities of infidelity' were 'fearlessly announced'. Its use now is radically different: as Altick and Wright note, 'Allibone . . . has a wealth of out-of-the-way information on third-and tenth-rate writers that is collected nowhere else'. The arrangement is alphabetical by author. A further thirty seven thousand articles on authors was supplied by John Foster Kirk's *A supplement to Allibone's Critical dictionary* (Philidelphia, Lippincott, 2 vols, 1891).

Another nineteenth century bibliographical work which, though not usually ranked as important as Watt, Lowndes or Allibone, is cited occasionally is William Carew Hazlitt's *Handbook to the popular, poetical and dramatic literature of Great Britain, from the invention of printing to the Restoration* (London, J R Smith, 1867); this was revised and supplemented by the same author's *Bibliographical collections and notes on early English Literature, 1474-1700* (London, Quaritch, 6 vols, 1876-1903), and by G J Gray's *General index to Hazlitt's Handbook and his Bibliographical collections (1867-1889)* (London, Quaritch, 1893). Again the scale is massive (many thousands of titles being listed and annotated), and again a modern reprint is available (from Burt Franklin, 1961).

There is an incontestable short-list of works which are the great monuments of English scholarship: the *Oxford English dictionary,* the British Museum catalogue, and the *Dictionary of national biography,* are of that number. Another is *The Cambridge bibliography of English literature,* edited by F W Bateson (Cambridge, Cambridge UP, 4 vols, 1940; Supplement, edited by G Watson, Cambridge, 1957), which is a descendant of *The Cambridge history of English literature,* 'supplying a modern equivalent' to its chapter bibliographies. The volumes of the work are arranged by period as follows: vol 1, 600-1660 (in three sections, Anglo-Saxon, Middle English, and Renaissance to Restoration); vol 2, 1660-1800; vol 3, 1800-1900. The fourth volume contains the index. Within each period, following an introduction which provides the intellectual, social and political background to the literary history, subdivision is by form. As its title indicates, this work is primarily a literary bibliography, but it does claim that 'no type of printed book, from the chapbook to the scientific treatise, from the collection of hymns to the gift-book, from the schoolboy's "crib" to the treatise on whist, has been altogether neglected'; it also claims to have 'recorded more fully than in any previous publication' newspapers and magazines. In its entries, it reproduces the wording and spelling of the title-page of the first edition; follows the date of the first edition with the dates of editions and translations of the subsequent fifty years; gives details of the more important or convenient modern editions and reprints; and notes briefly changes of title and revisions of the text. It attempts to include all important critical material, though it is less concerned with the biographical side if that information is readily available in the *Dictionary of national biography.* The *Annual bibliography of English language and literature* is to be regarded as supplementing it. Now in course of publication is *The New Cambridge bibliography of English literature,* under the editorship of George Watson. Vol 3, 1800-1900, appeared in 1969, and will be followed by vol 2, 1660-1800, and then by vol 1, 600-1660; vol 4, edited by Ian Willison, will cover 1900-1950; and finally, in a fifth volume, there will be a comprehensive analytical index to the whole work. The scope and essential character of the original *CBEL* will be retained, the aim of the new edition being merely to update and refine.

Clark Sutherland Northup's *A register of bibliographies of the English language and literature* (New Haven, Yale UP, 1925) aims, if not at completeness, certainly at fullness. It is in two parts, general (pp 9-33), and individual authors and topics (pp 34-417). The topics—for example, emblems, hymns and prayers, incunabula, printing and publishing, translations—range from the very small to the very large. Entries are often briefly annotated. As regards its scope, the *Introduction* points out that there are many general reference works which are of use to the student of English though not specifically connected with his subject, and cites many under such headings as: bibliographies of bibliographies, general bibliographies, catalogues of libraries, incunabula, manuscripts, learned societies and privately printed books, reference books, best books, printers and book-sellers, trade catalogues, periodicals, reviews, history and biography, dissertations. The impression the user derives from this is a fair one: Northup is a large, solemn, grubbing work; Esdaile characterizes it as 'almost too laborious', and in surveying its contents is driven to employ the adjectives 'irrelevant' and 'indiscriminate'. This judgment is too severe, in that any compilation on this scale runs the risk of being uncritical in its deliberate attempt to be as full as possible. Northup's work is continued by Nathan Van Patten's *An index to bibliographies and bibliographical contributions relating to the work of American and British authors, 1923-1932* (Stanford, Calif, Stanford UP, 1934).

Northup mentions the use of bibliographies of bibliographies to the student of English: the great name in the field here, of course, is Theodore Besterman, whose *A world bibliography of bibliographies* (Lausanne, Societas Bibliographica, 4th ed, 5 vols, 1965-66) records about one hundred and seventeen thousand volumes of bibliography in more than forty languages, and arranges them under approximately sixteen thousand headings and sub-headings. It is, as he claims, 'inclusive of all subjects, periods and languages'. The subject headings are in alphabetical order, and under each, the entries are set out in chronological order by date of publication. The fifth volume provides a comprehensive index of authors and subjects. This bibliography restricts its coverage to bibliographies published separately, a fact which must be borne in mind especially since many useful bibliographies appear, for example, in periodicals.

Further, Besterman excludes all general library catalogues, though he does record catalogues of special libraries or of special sections of general libraries. *A world bibliography of bibliographies* has been Besterman's chief preoccupation for thirty years and deserves to be regarded as a major work: the English specialist need only look under the heading *English literature* to be impressed. This is sub-divided into nine categories: Bibliographies and history; Periodicals; Writings on English literature; Manuscripts; General; Select; Periods; Translations, etc; Miscellaneous. There are the related headings *American literature, Canadian literature, Australian literature,* and so on; form headings such as *Poetry, Fiction,* and *Drama and stage,* which are sub-divided by country; and personal headings for individual authors.

A bibliography of bibliographies concerned solely with English literature is T H Howard-Hill's *Bibliography of British literary bibliographies* (Oxford, Clarendon P, 1969). This is the first volume of an *Index to British literary bibliography,* and its aim is to record all post-1890 publications in English which ' list the printed works of British writers, which list and describe the works published in Britain from 1475 to the present day, whether generally or classified by period, or literary form or genre, or which describe English works dealing with particular subjects '. The second volume of the *Index* deals exclusively with bibliographies of and bibliographical work on Shakespeare. A third volume will complete the work and contain a comprehensive index to the whole (though each volume will also be separately indexed). The first volume has 5,219 numbered entries; these comprise books, parts of books, and periodical articles. The contents are grouped as follows: General and bibliographies of and guides to British literature; General and period bibliographies; Regional bibliographies; Presses and printing; Forms and genres; Subjects (for example, Alchemy, Boxing, Law); and Authors. As a whole, this bibliography is poorly and ambiguously organized, and its coverage (though extensive) is capricious rather than systematic; in the words of a reviewer (Mrs L M Harrison, *Library Association record,* May 1969), it is a ' rich mine of information ' (especially with regard to bibliographies of individual authors) but those who use it ' will have to do a fair amount of unnecessary digging to exploit it fully '.

Samuel Halkett and John Laing's *Dictionary of anonymous and pseudonymous English literature* (new ed, by James Kennedy, W A Smith, and A F Johnson; Edinburgh, Oliver & Boyd, 9 vols, 1926-62) was, as its *Preface* states, ' the product of at least seventy five years of unbroken research ', and in its own special field ranks as the major bibliography. Anonymous and pseudonymous works are arranged alphabetically by title; the name of the author is added in square brackets; and finally, reference is made to the authority for the attribution. The main sequence is contained in vols 1-6; vol 6 also contains a supplement; vol 7 is made up of an index of authors, an index of initials and pseudonyms, and a very brief second supplement; vol 8 covers the anonymous and pseudonymous publications of the period 1900-1950; and vol 9 contains additions to the period before 1900, and many additional items for the first half of the twentieth century.

Though a librarian relies heavily on major bibliographies, and on bibliographies of bibliographies, more important to him still are the catalogues of major libraries: in particular, those of the British Museum and the Library of Congress. Without the British Museum's *General catalogue of printed books* (photolithographic edition to 1955, London, 263 vols, 1959-1966; *Ten year supplement 1956-65*, 50 vols, 1968) he would indeed be lost. Its volumes recording the great national collection constitute the major bibliographical tool for any large library in this country. The contents of a main entry are itemized in the *Rules for compiling the catalogues of printed books, maps and music in the British Museum* (rev ed, 1936):

1) A *Heading*.
2) A *Description* of the contents of the book.
3) An *Imprint*.
4) If necessary, a *Note*.

This is followed by the example:

1) LANDOR (Walter Savage).
2) Imaginary Conversations of Greeks and Romans. pp viii, 492.
3) *Edward Moxon: London, 1853. 8°*.

A second example gives as an illustration of a *Note: One of twenty-five copies printed on Japanese vellum.*

The standard of the British Museum catalogue's accuracy and reliability is very high. Not so high is that of the Library of Congress catalogue, the United States national equivalent. The publication of this catalogue in printed book form is complicated enough in itself, because since the catalogue is the result of work performed by an agency of the US Government it therefore ranks as a government publication and as such is in the public domain. Thus any firm wishing to reprint any segment or sequential combination of the Library of Congress catalogue cannot be prevented from doing so. Publication in printed book form was first projected in 1941, when a committee of the Association of Research Libraries sponsored the idea of reproducing a depository catalogue of Library of Congress cards; the outcome of this was *A catalog of books represented by Library of Congress printed cards issued to July 31, 1942,* the 167 volumes of which (reproducing approximately 1,900,000 cards) were published in 1946 by Edwards, Ann Arbor, Michigan. This was followed by two supplementary sets of volumes, covering 1942-1947 (42 vols, 1948) and 1948-1952 (24 vols, 1953). In 1958 was published the *National union catalog,* its twenty eight volumes covering the period 1953-57; the innovation here was that the catalogue now included not only books represented by Library of Congress printed cards but also those reported by five hundred or so other North American libraries. A supplement to the *National union catalog* was subsequently published, covering the period 1958-1962 (54 vols, 1963); and before this, in 1961, appeared the *National union catalog, 1952-1955 imprints,* listing titles previously included in earlier catalogues but with additional locations, as well as newly reported titles, many not represented by Library of Congress cards. To complicate the picture further, the Gale Research Company has produced a ' master cumulation ' of the Library of Congress and National Union Catalog author lists 1942-1962; and since 1968 the firm of Mansell has been publishing *The national union catalog, pre-1956 imprints: a cumulative author list representing Library of Congress printed cards and titles reported by other American libraries,* of which 144 volumes have appeared so far (April, 1971), reaching the letter D in the alphabetical sequence of authors. Inaccuracies and inconsistencies are plentiful in all the foregoing series, but they do offer a vast amount of practical help to the working librarian. The plethora of supplements (and the publication of current monthly, quarterly and annual issues, *see* p 46) at least have the merit of keeping the catalogue up-to-date; and the full entries provide the librarian with most of the bibliographical information he is likely to need. The last can be illustrated by itemization of the entry given in the Library of Congress catalogue for the Landor example used above:

1) Author: Landor, Walter Savage, 1775-1864.
2) Title: Imaginary conversations of Greeks and Romans. By Walter Savage Landor.
3) Imprint: London, E. Moxon, 1853.
4) Collation: viii, 492 p. 19½ cm.
5) Notes: First edition.
        Imperfect: half-title wanting.
6) Subject heading: Imaginary conversations.
7) Class-mark: PR 4872. I3 1853.

Here the librarian is given complete cataloguing information; a class-mark to use as it stands, or merely as a classificatory diagnosis of the book's subject; and a standard subject heading if he needs it.

Other library catalogues are plainly lesser in importance than these, but most fair-sized libraries find a place for the catalogue of the London Library (2 vols, 1913-14; Supplements, 1913-50, 3 vols) and that of the Edinburgh University Library (3 vols, 1918-23): the first has over 500,000 entries and is strong in literature, and the second, of course, features Scottish literature particularly. The *Catalogue of books in the John Rylands Library* (Manchester, 3 vols, 1899), edited by Edward Gordon Duff, which is concerned with books printed to the end of the year 1640, and Thomas James Wise's *The Ashley Library: a catalogue of printed books, manuscripts and autograph letters* (London, 11 vols, 1922-36), which gives full bibliographical descriptions mostly of first editions of English literary works, are equally famous.

One of the notable things of our time has been the growth and influence of American literature. It would be nonsense now to offer an English literature collection without including in it a strong representation of American authors. It follows that there is therefore a need for comprehensive bibliographies in this field. The famous names here are Sabin, Evans, Blanck and Spiller.

Joseph Sabin's *A dictionary of books relating to America, from its discovery to the present time* (New York, 29 vols, 1868-1936; reprinted in 15 vols, Amsterdam, Israel, 1961-2) is better known by its half-title *Bibliotheca Americana*. It was begun by Sabin, the result of ' some fifteen years of research ', continued by Wilberforce Eames, and completed by R W G Vail for the Bibliographical Society of America. In appearance and layout, it looks very old-fashioned, but it is a standard work. The arrangement is alpha-betical by author, and under each the works are listed by title, again alphabetically. A collation is given for each work, and each has a serial number. The last serial number is 106413, but as the *Introduction* to the final volume notes: ' thousands of these serial numbers represent not one but many titles or editions; in some cases dozens of editions appear in the main entries or the notes of a single number. It is therefore probable that well over a quarter of a million different publications appear in the Dictionary as well as the location in the world's great libraries of not far from a million copies.' As the dictionary progressed, its scope was further and further reduced in order that it might eventually be finished: for example, in 1932, it was decided not to list general poetry, drama and fiction after 1800.

Charles Evans's *American bibliography: a chronological diction-ary of all books, pamphlets and periodical publications printed in the United States of America from the genesis of printing in 1639 down to and including the year 1820* (Chicago, 13 vols and index, 1903-59) lists 39,162 items, and is the standard bibliography of early American publications. The arrangement is chronological and the bibliographical descriptions are full and exact. Each author's full names are given, and his birth and death dates also. Each work, or edition, described has a serial number; and locations in libraries, and auction values, are noted. In each of the thirteen volumes there is an index of authors, a classified subject-index, and a list of printers and publishers: and since this meant that searching Evans might involve consulting each of the thirteen volumes, a fourteenth volume has been supplied by Roger Pattrell Bristol which provides an author-title index to the whole work. Even though Evans even-tually lowered his sights to 1800, instead of 1820, the project still took him thirty five years. It was a single-handed labour, and a human note is supplied by Clifford K Shipton, who completed the

29

thirteenth volume, in his description of the technical side of Evans's work: 'He wrote his notes with a very fine pen on the backs of halved three-by-five library cards and packed them neatly into corset boxes which he could carry around under his arm'. Shipton's account of Evans makes this great bibliographer's name an automatic candidate for any bibliographical roll of honour.

The main interest of Jacob Blanck in his *Bibliography of American literature* (vol 1-, New Haven, Yale UP, 1955-) is 'to include all first editions, chronologically arranged, of each author' from the time of the Revolution: that is, American literature of the past 150 years, though excluding authors who died after 1930. The authors are alphabetically arranged, and the items are numbered. Blanck is not evaluative: 'to the bibliographer a titanic classic is no more important than the poorest production of the least talented author'. As befits its publication on behalf of the Bibliographical Society of America, Blanck provides real 'bibliography': the physical description of items—details of pagination, type of paper, size of leaf, signatures, binding, illustrations, and location of copies. The volume most recently published, vol 5 (1969), reaches Henry Wadsworth Longfellow and the 12,943rd entry. The completed work will be in eight or nine volumes, and will contain approximately 35,000 numbered entries covering some 300 authors.

The most practical comprehensive bibliography of American literature is provided in the second volume of the *Literary history of the United States* by Robert E Spiller and others (New York, Macmillan, 3rd ed rev, 2 vols, 1963). If the librarian of a collection of literature in English could afford only one work on American literature, this would have to be it. The first volume covers the history of American literature from colonial days to 'Since 1945', and its 1,511 pages are the work of an eminent group of scholars. The second volume, the bibliography volume, is equally massive, since the third edition is a combination of the original 1948 volume of 790 pages and the 1959 supplement of 239 pages; one is printed after the other, and only a new index links them. The contents of this bibliography are arranged in four groups:

Guide to resources
Bibliographies: Literature and culture

Bibliographies: Movements and influences

Bibliographies: Individual authors.

The last group is alphabetically arranged, and deals with 207 authors. Under each section and sub-section of this packed work, the presentation is briefly narrative, informative, and evaluative.

The best-known name in the bibliography of Canadian literature is Marie Tremaine, whose *A bibliography of Canadian imprints, 1751-1800* (Toronto, Toronto UP, 1952) lists 1,204 books, pamphlets, leaflets, broadsides, handbills and pictorial publications, arranging them chronologically year by year. Newspapers and magazines are also dealt with. For every item there is a full bibliographical description: heading, transcript of title, collation, contents, notes, and a record of copies located. A point worth noting is that all these items have been covered by a programme of micro-filming: the Canadian Library Association has been responsible for the micro-filming of newspapers, and the Canadian Bibliographic Centre for the micro-filming of the remainder.

A larger, brisker compilation is Reginald Eyre Watters's *A check list of Canadian literature and background materials, 1628-1950* (Toronto, Toronto UP, 1959), prepared on behalf of the Humanities Research Council of Canada. Brisker, because the compilation was done over a period of seven years from library catalogues, accepting their by no means uniform bibliographical data, the aim being to produce *something*, rather than stalling in an attempt to achieve perfection. Its sub-title describes it as being 'a comprehensive list of the books which constitute Canadian literature written in English, together with a selective list of other books by Canadian authors which reveal the backgrounds of that literature'; consequently, the 12,000 books listed are arranged in two groups: Part I 'attempts to record all known titles in the recognized forms of poetry, fiction, and drama that were produced by English-speaking Canadians' without applying any qualitative evaluation of these writings, and Part II is 'a more or less selective listing of books by Canadians which seem likely to be of value to anyone studying the literature or culture of Canada'. Watters made two physical requirements in regard to the books he set out to list: separate publication, and more than eight or nine pages in length. Locations are given, and there are two indexes: one of anonymous titles, and one of authors' names, initials and pseudonyms. Watters has also, with Inglis F Bell, compiled *On Canadian literature, 1806-1960: a check-list of articles, books and theses on English-Canadian literature, its authors and language* (Toronto, Toronto UP, 1966), the first part of which covers broad topics (for example, literary criticism, folklore), and the second, individual authors. It cites from some 100 periodicals, and may therefore be regarded as the Canadian equivalent of Lewis Leary's *Articles on American literature* (see chapter IX).

For a serious study of Canadian literature, Raymond Tanghe's *Bibliography of Canadian bibliographies* (published in association with the Bibliographical Society of Canada by Toronto UP, 1960; Supplements, 1962, 1964) is indispensable. It is a sound, professional listing of about 1,665 bibliographies, arranged according to their main subject (for example, religion, education, linguistics, literature, history). Before these various large subject groups, there are preliminary sections dealing with general bibliographies, current bibliographies, collective bibliographies, author bibliographies, and newspapers and reviews.

Watters's Canadian *Check-list* was inspired by that dealing with the literature of Australia by Edmund Morris Miller: *Australian literature: a bibliography to 1938* (extended to 1950, edited, with a historical outline and descriptive commentaries, by F T Macartney, Sydney, Angus & Robertson, 1956). This is arranged alphabetically by author, and gives biographical and critical information on the more important writers.

Miller deals with literature only, and if a guide to all Australian material is required, the bibliography to use is J A Ferguson's *Bibliography of Australia* (in progress, Sydney, Angus & Robertson, 1941-), the volumes of which are divided into the following periods: 1784-1830; 1831-38; 1839-45; 1846-50; and 1851-1900. The basic arrangement is by year of publication, within which authors are listed alphabetically. The entries are numbered, and locations of copies are given.

Finally, there is the bibliography of New Zealand. T M Hocken's great *Bibliography of the literature relating to New Zealand* (Wellington, Mackay, 1909; Supplement, by A H Johnstone, Auckland, Whitcombe & Tombs, 1927) will eventually be replaced by vol 1 (covering publications up to and including 1889) of the *New Zealand national bibliography to the year 1960.* This latter work, edited by A G Bagnall, is planned to comprise five volumes; vol 1 has already been mentioned, vols 2-4 will cover the period 1890-1960 in an alphabetical sequence of authors, and vol 5 will consist of an index and supplementary material. So far only vol 2, covering A-M of the alphabetical sequence, has been published (Wellington, Government Printer, 1970).

CHAPTER IV

Period, form, author, and current bibliographies

IN A FIELD as vast as literature in English, specialization is inevitable. After all, to become an authority on Chaucer or Shakespeare or Milton is one lifetime's work. If the name of a literary scholar of eminence is not linked with a particular author, as John Butt's is with Pope, then it is linked with a period, as David Nichol Smith's is with the eighteenth century, or with a form, as Allardyce Nicoll's is with drama. Bibliography is no different, and for the various periods and forms, and for many individual authors, specialized bibliographies exist. In addition, there is the bibliography of current literary output.

PERIOD BIBLIOGRAPHIES

For the bibliography of the literature of the Anglo-Saxon period, W L Renwick and Harold Orton's *The beginnings of English literature to Skelton, 1509* (2nd ed, 1952) is excellent. This volume is one of the *Introductions to English literature* series described in chapter II and may serve to remind the librarian that, of course, important period bibliographies are to be found in such series and multi-volume works: two others are Ford's *Guide to English literature,* also mentioned in chapter II, and the *Oxford history of English literature* (see chapter V). Manuscripts of the Anglo-Saxon period are described in N R Ker's 567-page *Catalogue of manuscripts containing Anglo-Saxon* (Oxford, Clarendon P, 1957), and their locations given. Ker's book deals with all categories of Anglo-Saxon: for the more strictly literary and linguistic there is Arthur H Heusinkveld and Edwin J Bashe's *A bibliographical guide to Old English* (vol II, no 5, of *University of Iowa humanistic studies,* Iowa, 1931), which lists 'the most important literary and linguistic monuments of the period ', and also, the bibliographical tools most ' necessary and useful '.

'Indispensable if uninspiring' is Bateson's description of the standard bibliography of Middle English: John Edwin Wells's *A manual of the writings in Middle English, 1050-1400* (New Haven, Yale UP, 1916), with its nine supplements (1919-51). Its preface records that the work aims ' to treat all the extant writings in print, from single lines to the most extensive pieces ', and that it ' groups each piece with the others of its kind; indicates its probable date . . . its MS or MSS . . . its form and extent . . . the dialect in which it was first composed . . . its source or sources . . . comments on each longer production, with an abstract of its contents; and supplies a bibliography for each composition '. *A manual of the writings in Middle English, 1050-1500* (fasc 1-, New Haven, Connecticut Academy of Arts and Sciences, 1967-), edited by J Burke Severs, is a rewriting and expansion of Wells's work, embracing the literature of the fifteenth century as well as the three and a half earlier centuries. Another bibliography of the period is *A bibliography of Middle English texts,* compiled by Margaret S Ogden and others (Ann Arbor, Michigan UP, 1954), which, in the form of 8,883 5×8 inch cards, was originally the bibliographical basis of Kurath's *Middle English dictionary* (see chapter VII). It covers texts, text editions, and manuscripts.

For the fifteenth century, there is Lena Lucile Tucker and Allen Rogers Benham's *A bibliography of fifteenth century literature* (vol 2, no 3 of *University of Washington publications in language and literature,* Seattle, 1928), which has the sub-title ' with special reference to the history of English culture ', so that preceding the main literary part of the work there are bibliographical treatments of the political, social, economic, cultural, and linguistic backgrounds. Books and articles are covered, with brief informative annotations. H S Bennett's *Chaucer and the fifteenth century (Oxford history of English literature,* vol 2, pt 1, 1947) has been praised by Bateson as containing ' the fullest list of fifteenth-century writings in English '.

The next period's bibliography is recorded in A W Pollard and G R Redgrave's *A short-title catalogue of books printed in England, Scotland, and Ireland, and of English books printed abroad, 1475-*

1640 (London, Bibliographical Society, 1926). What this work aims to list, of course, is the entire output of the period, not just the works of literature. Abridged entries are given for actual copies, with locations, and the entries are numbered. The listing is continued in an identical way by Donald G Wing's *Short-title catalogue of books . . . 1641-1700* (New York, Index Society, 3 vols, 1945-51). Paul G Morrison has produced an index of printers, publishers and booksellers in Pollard and Redgrave (Charlottesville, Bibliographical Society of Virginia, 1950), and one for Wing (1955). *A finding-list of English books to 1640 in libraries in the British Isles* (Durham, Council of the Durham Colleges, 1958) has been compiled by David Ramage, to supplement the locations supplied in Pollard and Redgrave; similarly, for the United States, there is William Warner Bishop's *A checklist of American copies of ' Short-title catalogue ' books* (Ann Arbor, Michigan UP, 2nd ed, 1950); and Donald Wing has compiled *A gallery of ghosts: books published between 1641-1700 not found in the Short-title catalogue* (New York, Modern Languages Association, 1967).

For the eighteenth century there is *English literature, 1660-1800: a bibliography of modern studies,* compiled for the *Philological quarterly* by Ronald S Crane, Louis I Bredvold, Richmond P Bond, Arthur Friedman, and Louis A Landa (Princeton, Princeton UP, 1950-1962). Vol I covers modern studies 1926-1938; vol 2, 1939-1950; vol 3, 1951-1956; and vol 4, 1957-1960. For each year the significant books and articles, grouped under headings such as ' Bibliographical aids ', ' General studies ', ' Studies of authors ', ' Studies relating to the political and social environment ', and ' Studies relating to the continental background ', are listed and critically appraised. *Seven XVIIIth century bibliographies,* by Iolo A Williams (London, Dulau, 1924), covers Akenside, Armstrong, Churchill, Collins, Goldsmith, Shenstone and Sheridan. For five of these there is an essay as well as a bibliography, but for Goldsmith and Sheridan a bibliography only : because, says Williams, an essay on these much written-about writers ' would be needless and presumptuous '. The bibliographies are bibliographies of first editions, giving a transcript of title-page, size, collation, and pagination. The first part of James Edward Tobin's *Eighteeenth century English literature and its cultural background: a bibliography* (New York,

Fordham UP, 1939), deals with the cultural and critical background; the second gives bibliographies of individual authors. Entries are brief and annotated.

For the nineteenth century, from 1801 and still continuing, there is the *English catalogue* (London, Publishers' Circular, 1914-), with entries under author, title, and subject, in one alphabet. Size, price, month and year of publication, and publisher, are given. This is a tiresome and unreliable series of volumes, but in many instances, the librarian has no alternative to it; though from 1874 there is Whitaker's *The reference catalogue of current literature. Bibliographies of studies in Victorian literature for the ten years 1955-1965,* ed by R C Slack (Urbana Chicago, Ill, University of Illinois P, 1967) comprises 7,922 entries listed originally in the periodicals *Modern philology* (1956-57) and *Victorian studies* (1958-65). Bridging the nineteenth and twentieth centuries is *English literature in transition* (Lafayette, Ind, Purdue University, 1963; previously, *English fiction in transition,* 1957-), which is devoted to scholarship on the period 1880-1920 and appears five times a year in duplicated typescript (back numbers are available in Kraus reprints).

The earlier part of the present century is treated in Fred Benjamin Millett's *Contemporary British literature* (3rd ed, based on the 2nd ed by J M Manly and Edith Rickert, London, Harrap, 1935), which is made up of a critical survey (pp 1-110), 232 author bibliographies alphabetically arranged, a brief (three pages) select bibliography of contemporary social, political and literary history, and then ' classified indexes '—that is, authors listed under categories such as ' Critics ', ' Dramatists ', ' Poets '. *Twentieth century British literature: a reference guide and bibliography* (New York, Ungar, 1968), compiled and edited by Ruth Z Temple, with the assistance of Martin Tucker for the author bibliographies, is a bibliographical guide proper, divided into two parts; the first deals with bibliographies, biographical sources, reference books, journals, histories and studies of modern literature, autobiographies and diaries, collections of essays, criticism, and the three main genres (drama, novel, poetry), while the second part lists contemporary authors alphabetically, giving for each a list of works and noting some critical and biographical studies.

Form bibliographies are as numerous as period bibliographies : poetry, drama and prose are all adequately covered.

A conspectus of English poetry was provided in 1947 by a National Book League exhibition of works of the English poets. John Hayward prepared the catalogue, *English poetry: a catalogue of first and early editions from Chaucer to the present day*. Titles are arranged chronologically, and fully described. Though most of the poets were represented only by a single volume, either by their first publication or by their best-known work, 346 items are recorded.

Middle English poetry has been well served by Carleton Brown's *A register of Middle English religious and didactic verse* (Oxford, Bibliographical Society, 2 vols, 1916-20), the first part of which is a list of all known manuscript material arranged in the order of the manuscripts in which it is preserved, and the second part comprises an index of first lines and an index of subjects and titles. In collaboration with Rossell Hope Robbins, Brown subsequently produced *The index of Middle English verse* (New York, Columbia UP, for the Index Society, 1943), which adds secular poetry and increases the *Register's* 2,273 entries distributed in about 1,100 manuscripts to 4,365 entries in over 2,000 manuscripts; and a *Supplement* (Lexington, Kentucky UP, 1966) by Robbins and John L Cutler expands 2,300 of the original 4,365 entries and adds 1,500 new entries. The Scots contribution to Middle English poetry is treated by William Geddie in *A bibliography of Middle Scots poets* (vol 61 of the Scottish Text Society, Edinburgh, 1912), which, after the general works, deals with the individual poets separately, including in its coverage biography and criticism.

Arthur E Case's *A bibliography of English poetical miscellanies, 1521-1750* (Oxford, Bibliographical Society, 1935), is chronologically arranged by the earliest known edition. Full bibliographical descriptions, and locations of copies are given.

For the nineteenth century, *The English Romantic poets: a review of research,* edited by Thomas M Raysor (New York, Modern Language Association, London, Oxford UP, rev ed, 1956), deals with the Romantic movement in general before dealing with Byron, Coleridge, Keats, Shelley and Wordsworth in particular. The style is narrative and evaluative, arranging the material in groups : bibliographies, editions, biographical studies, studies of ideas, general and miscellaneous criticism. *The Victorian poets: a guide to research,* edited by Frederic E Faverty (Cambridge, Mass, Harvard UP, 2nd ed, 1968), employs the same method, dealing with the subject generally, and then with Arnold, the Brownings, Clough, Fitzgerald, Hopkins, Swinburne and Tennyson, as well as with two groups: the Pre-Raphaelites, and the later Victorian poets.

Three reference works useful in this field are *Poetry explication,* compiled by Joseph M Kuntz (Denver, Swallow, rev ed, 1962) which indexes interpretations in books and periodicals; *Granger's index to poetry* (New York, Columbia UP, 5th ed, 1962; Supplement, 1967), the main volume of which indexes a total of 574 volumes of anthologies, mainly American, in three indexes: a title and first line index, an author index, and a subject index; and H Bruncken's *Subject index to poetry* (Chicago, American Library Association, 1940), which indexes 215 anthologies alphabetically by subject.

What was remarked in connection with period bibliographies, namely that in looking for specialized bibliography the librarian and literary student should not forget the appropriate parts of larger works, is particularly true of the bibliography of drama in respect of the histories of this form produced by Allardyce Nicoll (see chapter V), which contain authoritative bibliographies.

Alfred Harbage's *Annals of English drama, 975-1700* (Philadelphia, Pennsylvania UP, 1940; rev by S Schoenbaum, London, Methuen, 1964) is a record of all plays, extant or lost, chronologically arranged, and indexed by authors, titles, and dramatic companies. The book is set out double-paged, and the headings across the two pages are Date, Authors, Titles, Limits (of date), Type (rough classification of the play), Auspices (dramatic company which gave the first performance), First edition, and Last edition (latest modern edition): entries are set out under these headings in columns. G William Bergquist's *Three centuries of English and American plays* (New York, Hafner, 1963) is a checklist of approximately 5,350 British titles and 250 American ones, arranged alphabetically by dramatist. It is a by-product of a project originally suggested by Allardyce Nicoll: namely, that just such a collection of plays ought to be recorded in microprint. The Readex Microprint Corporation did just that, and this checklist is a guide to the collection, and gives also the 'Greg', and the 'Woodward and McManaway', numbers of the items.

'Greg' is Walter Wilson Greg's *A bibliography of the English printed drama to the Restoration* (London, Bibliographical Society, 4 vols, 1939-59), a massive work which gives full descriptions, and locations. Vol 1 is of Stationers' Company records for plays to 1616; vol 2 covers plays 1617-89, Latin plays and lost plays; vol 3 covers collections, and contains ancillary reference lists; vol 4 contains additions, corrections, and an index of titles. Two earlier compilations of Greg's are *A list of English plays written before 1643 and printed before 1700* (London, Bibliographical Society, 1900), and *A list of masques, pageants, etc* (Bibliographical Society, 1902); both are arranged alphabetically by author, giving transcriptions of the title-pages of works, but not collations. These two volumes are superseded by the major work. 'Woodward and McManaway' is *A check list of English plays, 1641-1700* (Chicago, Newberry Library, 1945; supplement, by Fredson Bowers, Charlottesville, University of Virginia, 1949), compiled by Gertrude Loop Woodward and James Gilmer McManaway, which, alphabetically by author, lists items briefly, and gives for them locations of copies in fifteen American libraries.

Two further period bibliographies of the form are *A bibliography of the Restoration drama,* by Montague Summers (London, Fortune P, 1950), which is alphabetically arranged by dramatist; and the very much more respectable and scholarly *Bibliography of medieval drama,* by Carl J Stratman (Berkeley, California UP, 1954). By medieval, Stratman means not so much the period as the type of drama: liturgical, mystery, miracle, morality, and interlude. He deals with general critical studies in book and periodical form, individual plays by edition, and critical studies of individual plays; and includes unpublished dissertations among the types of material he lists. Locations in the United States and Canada are given for every book mentioned, and the more important items in the bibliography are starred. Carl J Stratman has also compiled a *Bibliography of English printed tragedy, 1565-1900* (Carbondale, Southern Illinois UP, 1966), which gives the names of all English tragedies (1,483 of them, but excluding Shakespeare) which Father Stratman was able to locate whose first editions were printed between the dates specified. The entries are arranged alphabetically by dramatist, and under each tragedy the various editions are listed as well as the libraries which possess copies of specific editions; also supplied are brief but valuable notes referring to Pollard and Redgrave, Wing, Greg, and Woodward and McManaway numbers, Stationers' Register entries, the source of the play, its stage history, and so on.

A major work currently being published is *London stage, 1660-1800* (Carbondale, Southern Illinois UP, 1960-), the sub-title of which sufficiently describes its contents: 'A calendar of plays, entertainments and afterpieces, together with casts, box-receipts and contemporary comment, compiled from the playbills, newspapers and theatrical diaries of the period'. Blanch M Baker's *Theatre and allied arts* (New York, H W Wilson, 2nd ed, 1952) is a copiously annotated bibliography of about 6,000 items dealing with the history, criticism and technique of the drama and theatre and related arts and crafts. James Fullerton Arnott and John William Robinson's *English theatrical literature 1559-1900: a bibliography* (London, Society for Theatre Research, 1970) incorporates Robert W Lowe's *A bibliographical account of English theatrical literature* (1888); the latter, incidentally, having recently been reprinted (1966) uncritically by the Gale Research Company. Arnott and Robinson's revision of Lowe has taken some twenty years; their total number of entries (more than 5,000) is double that in Lowe's original work.

There are three indexes to this form which the librarian will find useful. John Henry Ottemiller's *Index to plays in collections* (New York, Scarecrow, 4th ed, 1964) is an author and title index and the collections are those published between 1900 and 1962; Dean H Keller's *An index to plays in a selected list of periodicals* (Kent, Ohio, Kent State University Library, 1960) indexes complete texts of plays; and I T E Firkin's *Index to plays, 1800-1926* (New York, Wilson, 1927; supplement, 1935), indexes all told about 11,000 plays either separately published or published in collections, periodicals and collected works. For the librarian in this country who wants an author catalogue of plays which gives details of the number of acts and characters, the setting, and the period, and the costume needed, there is the British Drama League Library's *The player's library* (London, Faber, 2nd ed, 1950; and three supplements, 1951-6).

41

2*

The bibliography of the novel should begin with Arundell Esdaile's *A list of English tales and prose romances printed before 1740* (London, Bibliographical Society, 1912), which is in two parts: 1475-1642, and 1643-1739, the outbreak of the Civil War being the dividing line. Within each, arrangement is alphabetical by author, and locations are given. In effect continuing Esdaile's work, but generally incomplete and unreliable, is Andrew Block's *The English novel, 1740-1850* (London, Dawsons, rev ed, 1961), arranged alphabetically by author and with an index of titles, and describing itself as ' including prose romances, short stories, and translations of foreign fiction '. Three other lists for the early period are Sterg O'Dell's *A chronological list of prose fiction in English printed in England and other countries, 1475-1640* (Cambridge, Massachusetts Institute of Technology, 1954), arranged chronologically with an author and anonymous title index, and giving locations of copies in sixty nine libraries; Charles C Mish's *English prose fiction, 1600-1700* (Charlottesville, University of Virginia Bibliographical Society, 3 vols, 1952), another chronological list, with very brief entries; and William Harlin McBurney's *A check list of English prose fiction, 1700-1739* (Cambridge, Mass, Harvard UP, 1960) which gives full descriptions and locations of 390 items.

The novel of the nineteenth century is handsomely served by Michael Sadleir's *XIX century fiction* (London, Constable, 2 vols, 1951), a bibilographical record based on Sadleir's own collection, and described with a collector's care. The main part of the first volume is ' an author-alphabet of first editions '. The second volume deals with ' yellow-backs ' (books issued in pictorial boards) and ' novelists' libraries ' (series such as Macmillan's *Illustrated standard novels* and Routledge's *Railway library*). The items are numbered serially, the last number being 3,761.

The English regional novel has been covered by Lucien Leclaire's *A general analytical bibliography of the regional novelists of the British Isles, 1800-1950* (Paris, Société d'Edition Les Belles Lettres, 1954), though since the English edition was limited to 235 copies this bibliography is not available readily everywhere. It is divided into three main periods—1800-1830, 1830-1870, and post-1870—and is indexed by author, by region, and by place-name. The entries are annotated.

Inglis F Bell and Donald Baird, in their *The English novel, 1578-1956: a checklist of twentieth-century criticisms* (Denver, Swallow, 1958) have provided an index to critical material in books and periodicals on the form, arranging it alphabetically by novelist. A similar treatment has been accorded American fiction in Donna Gerstenberger and George Hendrick's *The American novel, 1789-1959: a checklist of twentieth century criticism* (Denver, Swallow, 1961).

Bibliographies of American fiction itself are those by Lyle H Wright: *American fiction, 1774-1850* (San Marino, Calif, Huntington Library, 2nd rev ed, 1969), *American fiction, 1851-1875* (1957), and *American fiction, 1876-1900* (1966). The first has 2,772 numbered entries, the second 2,832, and the third 6,175. Only the first or earliest located edition of each title is recorded; entries indicate pagination and illustrations, giving bibliographical notes, and annotations on the topic of the particular novel. The basic arrangement is alphabetically by author.

The librarian working in a public lending library will find G B Cotton and A Glencross's *Cumulated fiction index 1945-1960* (London, Association of Assistant Librarians, 1960) useful in his dealings with readers who look to him for help in choosing what to read next, since it arranges over 25,000 fictional works by subject or type; useful also is F M Gardner's *Sequels* (London, Association of Assistant Librarians, 5th ed, 1967), the title of which is self-explanatory. E A Baker, the author of the standard English work on the history of the novel (see chapter V), compiled *A guide to historical fiction* (London, Routledge, 1914), which lists by country and then by period novels set in the past, and provides synopses of each; and in collaboration with James Packman also compiled *A guide to the best fiction* (London, Routledge, new ed, 1932), a comprehensive annotated list of English and American novels arranged alphabetically by author. For both the enthusiastic general reader and the librarian there is too G B Cotton and H M McGill's *Fiction guides* (London, Bingley, 1967), which covers bibliographies, indexes, guides to research, histories and an up-to-date selection of critical studies.

AUTHOR BIBLIOGRAPHIES

In the field of specialized bibliography, author bibliographies are a relatively new venture. Esdaile, in 1928, wrote that this branch of bibliography was 'practically the creation of the last or last two generations'. He goes on to say that the earliest he can recall are William Lee's of Defoe and George Offor's of Bunyan, that the 'most magnificent bibliography of an author ever produced' is Keynes's of Blake, and that Eleanor Prescott Hammond's bibliography of Chaucer raised the whole business to a 'higher power both of value and of difficulty'.

The presence of full-scale author bibliographies in an English collection is a token that the collection is serious in purpose. Author bibliographies are expensive and, very obviously, limited in use. In any number, they indicate that the collection must be aiming to cater for research in other directions too.

For the intensive study of an author such bibliographies are invaluable, since they will show the full extent and variety of the material, and will often also throw light on the literary, social and historical background. The main criteria by which author bibliographies should be judged are coverage, level, purpose, accuracy and arrangement. Coverage—is the bibliography selective or exhaustive? Level—for the scholar? for the general reader? Purpose—called for? fulfilled? Accuracy—compiler's authority, knowledge and experience? publisher's standing? Arrangement—apt? clear? easy to consult? annotated?

Lists of author bibliographies are not difficult to find. One certain source is the *Cambridge bibliography of English literature*. They are covered in Besterman's *A world bibliography of bibliographies;* and another full list is provided in vol 3 (Generalities, Languages, the Arts and Literature) of A J Walford's *Guide to reference material* (London, Library Association, 2nd ed, 3 vols, 1966-70).

There are also actual series of author bibliographies. The most notable currently are the Soho bibliographies published by Rupert Hart-Davis, under his personal guidance and with an advisory board of two librarians, the editor of *Book collector,* and Sotheby's bibliographical consultant. The subjects of these bibliographies are eminent figures in English and American literature of the past hundred years: Yeats, Housman, Beerbohm, Rupert Brooke, Sassoon, Joyce, Norman Douglas. Henry James, Virginia Woolf, Firbank, D H Lawrence, and the Sitwells, are examples. The material of each bibliography is arranged in three main categories: books and

44

pamphlets, contributions to books, contributions to periodicals. Within each category, titles are numbered in chronological sequence. Though there is plainly some effort to achieve a degree of conformity, this does not appear to extend to the method of bibliographical description. These bibliographies are expensive, no doubt because of the limited market for them, but in the words of the *Times literary supplement* reviewer, they exhibit ' taste and intelligence ' and ' make . . . out of bibliography, a visually satisfying page and a very handsome book '. Another series is that put out by Samuel A and Dorothy R Tannenbaum, *Elizabethan bibliographies* (New York, 1937-). There are about forty of these ' concise bibliographies ', which cover both the writer's work and material on him; and since 1967 (London, Nether Press) there have been supplements published recording more recent research. Two other series are the pamphlet series, *Writers and their work* (or, *British book news bibliographical series of supplements*), published for the British Council by Longmans since 1950, and *University of Minnesota pamphlets on American writers* (1959-). Both are becoming long series, especially the former; both are inexpensive but authoritative, combining a brief essay with a bibliography. In the first, scholars such as Tillyard have written on Milton, Ian Jack on Pope, Richard Hoggart on Auden; in the second, Schorer on Sinclair Lewis, Waggoner on Hawthorne, and Edel on James. Yet another useful series is Oliver and Boyd's *Writers and critics,* covering both English and American authors and supplying select bibliographies; about seventy of these have appeared since the first one on Ezra Pound. Indeed, stimulated no doubt by the growing demands of higher education, a large number of publishers—Evans, Macmillan, Routledge, Weidenfeld, for example—are now rushing out series of biographical/critical/bibliographical studies of major authors. Obviously such series vary considerably in merit, and only time will endorse—as in the case of *Writers and their work, University of Minnesota pamphlets on American writers,* and *Writers and critics* —or deny, their respective worth.

CURRENT BIBLIOGRAPHIES

The excellent *Bibliographic index,* produced by the H W Wilson Company of New York since 1937, may be regarded as shading author bibliography into current bibliography, because though it has recorded every author bibliography published since 1937 and is therefore invaluable in that field, its main value of course lies in the fact that it indexes *all* current bibliographies, whether published separately or whether published as part of something else. It is issued twice a year, and cumulates into annual and multi-annual volumes.

Of the kinds of bibliographies mentioned so far, current bibliographies are the most vital as far as a librarian is concerned. They are his life-line in the day to day selection and maintenance of stock.

In this country, since 1950, the chief current bibliography has been the *British national bibliography,* which, though an independent publication with its own Council, is edited from the British Museum, and is based on the copyright accessions to that library. It is a weekly list, cumulating monthly, and then three-, six-, nine-, and twelve-monthly; there are also five-year cumulated indexes of authors, titles, subjects and series. The entries are classified by the Decimal Classification ('Dewey') with an adapted notation and catalogued according to the Anglo-American code. Thus for the librarian, as far as British publications are concerned, it offers more or less everything he needs: current bibliography, cataloguing information, and subject diagnoses. In addition, it also offers a catalogue card service. The American national equivalent is the *National union catalog,* published in nine monthly issues, with three quarterly cumulations and an annual one. Since there is no quarterly cumulation for October-December, the monthly issues must be used until the annual cumulation is published, usually several months later. The monthly issues reproduce the cards prepared for works published during the current and past two years, while the quarterly and annual cumulations show all cards printed during the period, regardless of imprint date. The annual volumes cumulate quinquennially.

For all books published in English, that is, British books and American books and Commonwealth books also, there is the H W Wilson *Cumulative book index* (1928-), issued monthly and cumulating eventually into bound six-month, annual, two-year and five-year volumes. In one alphabetical sequence, it presents entries under author, title and subject. It is eminently accurate and reliable.

The same cannot be said of the well-known British trade list, Whitaker's *Cumulative book list* (1924-), the volumes of which are based on the *Bookseller* weekly and monthly lists. Whitaker's also produce *British books in print: the reference catalogue of current literature,* in two volumes: an authors volume and a titles volume. A similar work is the annual *Books in print,* published by the R R Bowker Company of New York, which has a companion volume, *Subject guide to books in print.*

Now, of course, all the foregoing are general lists. Dealing specifically with literature in English is the *Annual bibliography of English language and literature 1920-* edited for the Modern Humanities Research Association (Cambridge, 1921-), covering books, pamphlets, periodical articles, and book reviews. It is arranged in sections, and literature is first treated generally, and then by period. Whereas the *Annual bibliography* only lists, *The year's work in English studies, 1919-* (edited for the English Association, 1921-) has a running evaluative text, and though it covers less titles it is more up-to-date. It is arranged by period, and indexes authors, authors written about, and subjects. There is a separate chapter on American literature. The third great current bibliography of literature in English is the annual bibliography which has appeared in the American literary periodical *PMLA* (*Publications of the Modern Language Association of America*) since 1921. This is a massive piece of work, international in coverage; apart from an analytical table of contents, there is also a list of the periodicals indexed as part of it. With the listings for 1969, the *MLA international bibliography* appeared in a new format, quite separate from its parent journal *PMLA;* approximately 1,500 periodicals are now indexed. A relative newcomer, but a very useful one, is *Studies in English literature, 1500-1900,* a quarterly journal of historical and critical studies, published by Rice University, Houston, Texas, since 1961. The issues are arranged as follows:

Winter   — English renaissance
Spring   — Elizabethan and Jacobean drama
Summer — Restoration and eighteenth century
Autumn — Nineteenth century

What is relevant in the present context is that each issue contains a substantial critical survey of studies in its field published during the preceding twelve months. Librarians and others will find Richard A Gray's *Serial bibliographies in the humanities and social sciences* (Ann Arbor, Pierian P, 1969) very useful in revealing where other similar lists and surveys are to be found; Gray arranges his guide by the Dewey Decimal Classification, so that all items relevant to English studies can be found in the sections 410 (English language), 810 (American literature) and 820 (English literature).

For Canadian publications, there is *Canadiana: publications of Canadian interest noted by the National Library* (Ottawa, 1951-), published monthly and cumulating annually. Before this, there was annually *The Canadian catalogue of books published in Canada, about Canada, as well as those written by Canadians* (Toronto Public Libraries, 1923-50, covering 1921-49); for the period before this, Dorothea Douglas Tod and Audrey Cordingley's bilingual *A check-list of Canadian imprints 1900-1925* (Ottawa, Cloutier, 1950) may be consulted. A critical survey of the year's Canadian literature appears annually in the July issue of the *University of Toronto quarterly*: another annual list has appeared in *Canadian literature* since 1960, dealing with English-Canadian and French-Canadian publications in all fields, but not discussing them critically.

Australia is served by the *Australian national bibliography* (Canberra, National Library of Australia, 1961-), based on copyright items deposited in the National Library, which is issued monthly and cumulates annually. It replaces *Books published in Australia,* a monthly publication which used to cumulate into the *Annual Catalogue of Australian publications* (1936-60). New Zealand, similarly, has the *New Zealand national bibliography* (Wellington, National Library of New Zealand, 1967-), again monthly and again cumulating annually; this replaces *Current national bibliography,* which was issued by the National Library Centre, and *Copyright publications* (New Zealand, General Assembly Library, 1934-), an annual publication cumulating the monthly *Copyright list*.

CHAPTER V

Literary history, biography and criticism

LITERARY HISTORY—GENERAL : The contrast apparent between the two giants in the field of English literary history, between, that is, *The Cambridge history of English literature* (edited by A W Ward and A R Waller, Cambridge, Cambridge UP, 15 vols, 1907-27, reprinted without bibliographies 1932), and *The Oxford history of English literature* (edited by F P Wilson and B Dobrée, to be in 12 vols, Oxford, Clarendon P, 1945-), is satisfyingly mnemonic. It is not merely romancing to feel that their respective characters are mirrored in their actual physical appearance : the mellow, expansive red-brown volumes of the *CHEL* as compared with the trim, modern, dark blue ones of the *OHEL*.

Age, of course, has most to do with this. The *CHEL* was completed in 1916 (the index volume was published in 1927); the *OHEL* is still appearing. The expansiveness of the *CHEL* no doubt results from its being the more collaborative work of the two : there are many contributors to each volume. Each volume of the *OHEL,* on the other hand, is the work of one author. In coverage, the *CHEL* does not go beyond the nineteenth century; the *OHEL* brings us as far as Yeats, Joyce and Lawrence.

There are also two major differences in presentation. The reprinted *CHEL* is without bibliographies, and therefore must be supplemented by the *Cambridge bibliography,* whereas about one-third of each *OHEL* volume is taken up with bibliographies. And while *CHEL* has a one-volume overall index, the index of each *OHEL* volume must be consulted separately.

There is no question, of course, of choosing one of these works as opposed to the other. They are not alternatives. They are each sufficiently distinctive in character, and each sufficiently important, for both to demand a place in even the smallest of English collections.

A shorter history, but a much-praised one, is *A literary history of England,* edited by Albert Croll Baugh (London, Routledge, rev ed, 4 vols, 1967); this has been admired by commentators as dissimilar as F Seymour Smith and F W Bateson for its clarity, its comprehensiveness, and its reliable bibliographical information. Also collaborative, and now also in four volumes, is *A history of English literature,* edited by Hardin Craig (reprinted with additions and corrections, New York, Collier, 1962; original one-volume edition, New York, Oxford UP, 1950). The period up to 1485 is dealt with by George K Anderson, 1485-1660 by Craig himself, 1660-1798 by Louis I Bredvold, and 1798 to the first world war by Joseph Warren Beach. The eminence of these names may fairly be regarded as a guarantee of this work's worth.

Any library, in addition, needs one-volume histories: for portability, for ease of use, for conciseness of approach. There is a one-volume abridgment of *CHEL* by George Sampson, *The concise Cambridge history of English literature,* each chapter of which ‘ takes for its subject-matter the volume that bears its title and reference to the parent work is therefore easy ’. Paragraphs and sentences of the original have been incorporated, and most of the pruning has been done in the areas of literary sources and foreign affiliations. The most recent version of this (Cambridge, Cambridge UP, 3rd ed, 1970), by R C Churchill, contains a chapter on American literature and one on the mid-twentieth century literature of the English-speaking world. There is also George Saintsbury's one-volume *A short history of English literature* (London, Macmillan, 1898), which is still, in its author's own words, ‘ a storehouse of facts ’.

Earlier histories, still of use, which the librarian of an English collection may have inherited, are Henri Taine's *History of English literature* (in translation, Edinburgh, Edmonston & Douglas, 2 vols, 1871), and J J Jusserand's *A literary history of the English people, from the origins . . . to the Civil War* (in translation, London, Fisher Unwin, 1895-1909). Two other Frenchmen, Emile Legouis and Louis Cazamian, wrote *A history of English literature* more recently (first published in Paris in 1924, appearing in translation originally in 1926-7, and now in a revised edition from Dent, 1964), which is equally well known. Finally, in this matter of general literary histories, the reader should not forget the excellent guides mentioned in the chapter on selective bibliographies: the five-volume *Introductions to English literature* edited by Bonamy Dobrée, and the seven-volume *Guide to English literature* edited by Boris Ford.

LITERARY HISTORY—PERIODS

Histories of the various periods of English literature are numerous. For the Anglo-Saxon period, a short-list of histories would include George K Anderson's *The literature of the Anglo-Saxons* (rev ed, 1966), Stopford A Brooke's *English literature from the beginning to the Norman conquest* (1898) and *The history of early English literature* (2 vols, 1892), J Earle's *Anglo-Saxon literature* (1884), W P Ker's *The dark ages* (1904), Kenneth Sisam's *Studies in the history of Old English literature* (1883), P G Thomas's *English literature before Chaucer* (1924), E E Wardale's *Chapters on Old English literature* (1935), and C L Wrenn's *A study of Old English literature* (1967); for the Middle English period, R W Chambers's *On the continuity of English prose* (1932), Dorothy Everett's *Essays on Middle English literature* (1955), George Kane's *Middle English literature* (1951), W P Ker's *English literature: medieval* (1912), C S Lewis's *The allegory of love* (1936), Margaret Schlauch's *English medieval literature and its social foundations* (Warsaw, 1956), R M Wilson's *Early Middle English literature* (3rd ed, 1968), and the appropriate volumes of the *Oxford history* by Sir E K Chambers and H S Bennett.

Five studies of the Elizabethan and seventeenth-century periods which are always recommended are Hardin Craig's *The enchanted glass* (1936), George Saintsbury's *A history of Elizabethan literature* (1887), E M W Tillyard's *The Elizabethan world picture* (1943), C V Wedgwood's *Seventeenth-century English literature* (1950), and Basil Willey's *The seventeenth-century background* (1934).

The eighteenth century is served principally by Oliver Elton's *A survey of English literature, 1730-80* (2 vols, 1928) and Sir Leslie Stephen's *English literature and society in the eighteenth century* (1904), but there are also Alexandre Beljame's *Men of letters and the English public in the eighteenth century* (in translation, 1948), Austin Dobson's *Eighteenth-century vignettes* (three series, 1892-6)

51

and *Miscellanies* (two series, 1898-1901), *Essays on the eighteenth century presented to David Nichol Smith* (1945), George Saintsbury's *The peace of the Augustans* (1916), and Basil Willey's *The eighteenth-century background* (1940).

Oliver Elton's survey continued into the nineteenth century with *A survey of English literature, 1780-1830* (2 vols, 1912), and *A survey of English literature, 1830-1880* (2 vols, 1920); George Saintsbury also wrote on the nineteenth century, in *A history of nineteenth-century literature, 1780-1895* (1896); and Basil Willey has produced further studies, *Nineteenth-century studies* (1949) and *More nineteenth-century studies* (1956). G K Chesterton wrote on *The Victorian age in literature* (1913), and J H Buckley reviewed it critically in *The Victorian temper* (1951). Two useful guides to the period, both American in origin, are Ernest Bernbaum's *Guide through the Romantic movement* (2nd ed, 1949), and John Daniel Cooke and Lionel Stevenson's *English literature of the Victorian period* (1949).

The early twentieth century is treated in Frank Swinnerton's *The Georgian literary scene, 1910-35* (1935); and the twentieth century period in general by A C Ward in *Twentieth-century English literature, 1901-1960* (13th ed, 1964) and by the brilliant critic Edmund Wilson in *Axel's castle: a study of the imaginative literature of 1870-1930* (1931).

LITERARY HISTORY—POETRY

Histories of the separate genres are equally numerous. The best known large work on poetry is W J Courthope's *A history of English poetry* (6 vols, 1895-1910), but of course this is not to forget Dr Johnson's great '*Lives of the poets*' (10 vols, 1779-81, properly called *Prefaces biographical and critical to the works of the English poets*), nor the work by his contemporary, Thomas Warton, *The history of English poetry from the eleventh to the eighteenth century* (3 vols, 1774-81). A one-volume modern history is Sir Herbert Grierson and J C Smith's *A critical history of English poetry* (1947); and for the general reader there is James Reeves's *A short history of English poetry, 1340-1940* (London, Heinemann, 1961). Period studies of the genre are, for the Anglo-Saxon period, Charles W Kennedy's *The earliest English poetry* (1943) and W P

Ker's *Epic and romance* (2nd ed, 1908); for the Middle English period, John Speirs's *Medieval English poetry* (1957); for the Renaissance and seventeenth century, J M Berdan's *Early Tudor poetry, 1485-1547* (1920), Douglas Bush's *Mythology and the Renaissance tradition in English poetry* (1933), and Helen White's *The metaphysical poets* (1936); for the eighteenth century, James Sutherland's *A preface to eighteenth-century poetry* (1948) and *English satire* (1958); for the nineteenth century, Douglas Bush's *Mythology and the Romantic tradition in English poetry* (1937) and B Ifor Evan's *English poetry in the later nineteenth century* (1933); and for the twentieth century, there is F R Leavis's *New bearings in English poetry* (1950). Mention might also be made of *Scottish poetry: a critical survey,* edited by James Kinsley.

LITERARY HISTORY—DRAMA

Drama is treated comprehensively in Allardyce Nicoll's *A history of English drama, 1660-1900* (rev ed, 6 vols, 1952-9). Period studies of the form are, for the mediaeval period, Karl Young's classic *The drama of the medieval church* (2 vols, 1933), Sir E K Chambers's *The mediaeval stage* (2 vols, 1903), Hardin Craig's *English religious drama of the Middle Ages* (1955); for the Elizabethan and following period, Sir E K Chambers's *The Elizabethan stage* (4 vols, 1923), F E Schelling's *Elizabethan drama, 1558-1642* (2 vols, 1908), M C Bradbrook's *Themes and conventions of Elizabethan tragedy* (1935), and *The growth and structure of Elizabethan comedy* (1955), L C Knight's *Drama and society in the age of Jonson* (1937), Una Ellis-Fermor's *The Jacobean drama* (1936), and Gerald E Bentley's *The Jacobean and Caroline stage* (7 vols, 1941-68); for the Restoration period, Bonamy Dobrée's *Restoration comedy* (1924) and *Restoration tragedy* (1929); and for the nineteenth century, there is George Rowell's *The Victorian theatre: a survey* (1956).

LITERARY HISTORY—NOVEL

The definitive history of the novel is Ernest Albert Baker's *History of the English novel* (London, Witherby, 10 vols, 1924-39). An excellent two-volume introduction, though, is Arnold Kettle's *Introduction to the English novel* (2nd ed, 1967); and highly regarded one-volume histories are Walter Allen's *The English novel* (1954),

Walter Raleigh's *The English novel* (1891), Lionel Stevenson's *The English novel* (1960), and Ian Watt's *The rise of the novel* (1957). The last deals with Defoe. Richardson and Fielding; other period studies are J M S Tompkins's *The popular novel in England, 1770-1800* (1952), Kathleen Tillotson's *Novels of the eighteen-forties* (1954), and David Cecil's *Early Victorian novelists* (1934). An important research guide is *Victorian fiction*, edited by Lionel Stevenson (Cambridge, Mass, Harvard UP, 1964), which evaluates the mass of critical and scholarly work now available on the major novelists of the period.

LITERARY HISTORY—AMERICA, CANADA, AUSTRALIA, NEW ZEALAND

A collection of literature in English must cover American and Commonwealth literary history, too. The standard history of American literature, the *Literary history of the United states* by Robert E Spiller and others, has already been described in chapter III. Earlier, but still standard, is the *Cambridge history of American literature,* edited by W P Trent and others (New York, Putnam, 4 vols, 1918-21). Two one-volume histories are *The literature of the United* States by Marcus Cunliffe (3rd ed, 1967), and *The literature of the American people* by Arthur Hobson Quinn and others (1951). Period histories, for the earlier part, are Moses Coit Tyler's *A history of American literature, 1607-1765* (2 vols, 1878) and *The literary history of the American Revolution, 1763-1783* (2 vols, 1897), and Perry Miller's *The New England mind: from colony to province* (1953) and *The New England mind: the seventeenth century* (1939); for the nineteenth century, F O Matthiessen's *American renaissance* (1941); and for the twentieth century, Alfred Kazin's *On native grounds: an interpretation of modern American prose literature* (1942) and Heinrich Straumann's *American literature in the twentieth century* (1951).

Carl Frederick Klinck has edited a *Literary history of Canada* (Toronto UP, 1965), and the full-scale work on Australian literature is H M Green's *A history of Australian literature, pure and applied: a critical review of all forms of literature produced in Australia from the first books published after the arrival of the First Fleet until 1950, with short accounts of later publications up to 1960* (Sydney, Angus & Robertson, 2 vols, 1961). Green, who was Librarian of the University of Sydney, divides his book into four periods: 1789-1850, 1850-90, 1890-1923, and 1923-1950. Each period is again divided, into two parts, the first dealing with its pure literature and ending with its magazines and reviews, the second dealing with its applied literature (that is, history, economics, science, and so forth) and ending with its newspapers; and yet again within each of these two parts, the various kinds of literature are grouped: for example, poetry, drama, fiction, history. A shorter history, and a more rapidly readable one, is Cecil Hadgraft's *Australian literature: a critical account to 1955* (London, Heinemann, 1960).

Finally, for New Zealand, there is E H McCormick's *New Zealand literature: a survey* (London, Oxford UP, 1959); and supplementing this, Joan Stevens's *The New Zealand novel, 1860-1965* (Wellington, Reed, 2nd ed, 1966), since, as its author explains, McCormick was not able to deal with minor novelists and give detailed analyses of the work of major ones, having the whole of New Zealand literature to survey.

BIOGRAPHY

Works of literary biography are as necessary as works of literary history, but of course while literary history is most usually treated in its own right and not as part of general history, the same is not true of literary biography. The librarian of an English collection will find himself more often than not consulting works of general biography in his literary researches. An outstanding example of this will be the frequent use he will make of *The dictionary of national biography*, edited originally by Leslie Stephen, which had its inception at the beginning of the century and which is continued by supplements. This multi-volume work has already been referred to as one of the great monuments of British scholarship, and though intensive researchers are not always satisfied with the accuracy of its details (an index of corrections and alterations is maintained at the Institute of Historical Research, University of London, and these are published in the Institute's *Bulletin*), the *DNB* must still be regarded as the definitive biographical dictionary of ' all men and women of British or Irish race who have achieved any reasonable measure of distinction in any walk of life '. The qualification for entry in the *DNB*, in brief, is to be British, famous, and dead.

All the *DNB*'s articles are contributed, and signed, by persons considered to be expert on the life of the biographee; sources of information, and bibliographies, are given. The main run of volumes covers deceased persons up to 1900; the supplementary volumes bring the work down to 1950. Particularly valuable for British nineteenth-century biography is Frederic Boase's *Modern English biography* (Truro, Netherton & Worth, 6 vols, 1892-1921; reprinted, London, Cass, 6 vols, 1965), which contains some 30,000 short biographical sketches of persons who died between the years 1851-1900; indeed, its coverage of the period is better than that of the *DNB*. Most of the entries give the source of information, and Boase also notes the existence of portraits and photographs; he lists published works where relevant, and each of the volumes has a useful subject index.

For American literary figures, the *Dictionary of American biography* (New York, Scribner's, 22 vols, 1928-37), which aims to achieve the same standard as the *DNB,* is to be consulted. More comprehensive, since current volumes cover living people, but less scholarly, is *The national cyclopaedia of American biography* (New York, White, 1892-). For short biographies of many Canadian authors, the *Encyclopedia Canadiana* (Ottawa, Canadiana Company, 10 vols, 1957-8, reprinted and up-dated 1965) will be found useful; and in 1966 there appeared the first volume of the *Dictionary of Canadian biography* (Toronto, Toronto UP), which aims to supply full, accurate and concise biographies of all noteworthy inhabitants of the Dominion of Canada, exclusive of living persons, and which, unlike the *DNB,* is being organized by periods (vol 1 covering 1000-1700) rather than in one alphabetical sequence. For Australia there is now in progress the *Australian dictionary of biography* (Melbourne, Melbourne UP, 1966-) which, like the new Canadian biographical dictionary, also favours chronological division; two volumes are planned for the 1788-1850 period, four for the 1851-1890 period, and six for 1891-1938.

As well as by these larger works, the librarian of an English collection is also served by the one-volume universal biographical dictionaries, especially for quick reference. The three best-known are *Chambers's biographical dictionary* (Edinburgh, Chambers, new ed, 1961) with 15,000 entries; *Webster's biographical dictionary*

(Springfield, Mass, Merriam, 1953) with 40,000 entries; and A M Hyamson's *A dictionary of universal biography* (London, Routledge, 2nd ed, 1951) which gives only one-line entries and is really a finding-list of biographies contained in the larger biographical dictionaries and encyclopedias.

Dealing strictly and exclusively with literary biography, however, is *Everyman's dictionary of literary biography, English and American* (London, Dent, rev ed, 1960), a revised version by D C Browning of John W Cousin's *Biographical dictionary of English literature* (originally, 1910). This contains about 2,300 biographies, and covers ' low-brow ' as well as ' high-brow ' authors. It is compact, inexpensive, and very useful. A similar but more expensive work is *A dictionary of literature in the English language, from Chaucer to 1940* (Oxford, Pergamon P, 2 vols, 1970), edited by Robin Myers. Its aim is to provide ' bibliographical and biographical details of some 3,500 authors '; the entries are arranged alphabetically, and each contains full name and title, dates, biographical note, bibliographical sources used in compilation or suggested for further study, and a list of separately published literary works in chronological order; the second volume is an alphabetical index of the 60,000 titles found under author in the first volume. Works by living writers are listed up to February 1966, and in coverage Myers is as much interested in the detective novelist John Dickson Carr as in Daniel Defoe.

A familiar group of volumes on the shelves of most libraries are the biographical compilations by Stanley Jasspon Kunitz and Howard Haycraft: *Twentieth century authors* (New York, Wilson, 1942; 6th printing, 1966), with its *First supplement* (1955; 4th printing, 1967), *British authors of the nineteenth century* (1936; 6th printing, 1964), *British authors before 1800* (1952; 4th printing, 1965), and *American authors, 1600-1900* (1938; 7th printing, 1969). The style is informal and journalistic, but the articles are informative and are accompanied by portraits.

For American authors also, there is W J Burke and Will D Howe's *American authors and books, 1640 to the present day*, augmented and revised by Irving R Weiss (London, Vane, 1963). This is alphabetically arranged by author, and consists of concise entries giving dates of birth and death, description (for example,

'Episcopal clergyman, archaeologist, author '), and a list of works with dates. For modern American authors, there is Fred Benjamin Millett's *Contemporary American authors* (London, Harrap, 1940), which includes in addition to a critical survey of American literature, 219 bio-bibliographies. Millett, of course, produced a similar work for modern British literature (described in chapter IV). Also mentioned earlier, in chapter III, was Allibone's *Critical dictionary of English literature and British and American authors,* with its 46,000 literary biographies.

The Gale Research Company now produces semi-annually *Contemporary authors*, claiming to offer ' detailed personal information concerning more than 3,500 current authors each year '.

LITERARY CRITICISM

As well as works on literary history and biography, an English collection will also contain works on literary criticism. Some standard and important titles in this field are J W H Atkins's *English literary criticism* (1943-1951), the three volumes of which cover, respectively, the mediaeval phase, the renascence and the seventeenth and eighteenth centuries; René Wellek's *A history of modern criticism, 1750-1950* (vols 1-4, 1955-); Wellek and Austin Warren's *Theory of literature* (originally published 1949; 3rd ed, 1963); and William Wimsatt and Cleanth Brooks's *Literary criticism: a short history* (1957).

CHAPTER VI

Encyclopedias and reference works

ENCYCLOPEDIAS: To describe a work in any subject field as encyclopedic is to indicate that it treats every aspect of that field. Consequently, an encyclopedia of English literature may be expected to contain bibliographical and biographical information, and literary history; to identify real and fictitious persons appearing in literary works, and to give plots and descriptions of particular works; to describe literary forms, and to trace literary schools and movements; to define literary terms and to provide literary criticism; to deal with literary periodicals and literary societies; to indicate translations; and to relate literature in English to other literatures.

Though describing itself as a ' companion ' rather than an encyclopedia, *The Oxford companion to English literature,* edited by Sir Paul Harvey (Oxford, Clarendon P, 4th ed, 1967), is just such a work. Its two main elements, says its preface, are a list of English authors, literary works, and literary societies which have historical or present importance; and explanations of allusions containing a proper name (fictional and mythological characters, saints—' in short . . . every kind of celebrity '). Under an author's name, there is a concise collection of facts, especially dates, bearing on his life and literary activity; under a work, an indication of its nature and plot. One feature which a librarian will note and appreciate, is its usefulness in providing information on early literary periodicals.

A full-dress encyclopedia, not limited to literature in English only, is S H Steinberg's *Cassell's encyclopaedia of literature* (London, Cassell, 1953). This is the work of 217 specialist contributors; their names are given at the beginning of the first volume, along with the topics to which they contributed. There are three parts contained in the two volumes, each part alphabetically arranged. The first part provides histories of the literatures of the world, and articles on particular topics and forms: for example, bibliography, textual criticism, epigrams, classicism, poetry, novel. The second part gives biographies and bibliographies of authors who died before August 1 1914; and the third part gives biographies and bibliographies of authors who were living on August 1 1914, or who were born after that date. The entries in the third part are shorter than those in the second.

Laurie Magnus's *A dictionary of European literature* (London, Routledge, 2nd ed, 1927) aims, according to its preface, ' to provide, in a single volume, the information which students require complementary to a history of English literature or to the special study of a part of it '. The period covered is roughly the twelfth to the twentieth century: the only living authors (in 1927, that is) included are Thomas Hardy and Georg Brandes. There are articles on literary history and literary movements, and on literary terms; the biographical accounts of major and minor writers contain some bibliography. American literature is excluded, of course, but: ' Our own literature is admitted rather fully '.

William Rose Benet's *The reader's encyclopedia: an encyclopedia of world literature and the arts* (London, Harrap, 2nd ed, 1965) really is meant for the general reader, and not for the scholar. Its brief entries cover authors, titles, allusions, movements, literary terms, and characters. The origins of Benet's work lie in Ebenezer Cobham Brewer's justifiably famous *Dictionary of phrase and fable* (London, Cassell, 10th ed, 1967), which first appeared in 1870. *Brewer* contains most of the phrases and allusions one is likely to come across in ordinary reading. Under G, for example, he includes entries for 'All he touches turns to gold ', the Golden Fleece, the Golden Gate, Golgotha, Gondola, Good Samaritan, and Goodwin Sands: these give some idea of the range. For characters in English novels and plays, there is now William Freeman's *Dictionary of fictional characters* (London, Dent, 1963).

Joseph Twadell Shipley's *Dictionary of world literature: criticism, forms, technique,* first published in New York in 1943, was revised as *Dictionary of world literary terms: criticism, forms, technique* (London, Allen & Unwin, 1955, new edition 1971). Its preface describes it as ' a consideration of literary criticism, of literary schools, movements, techniques, forms and terms, of the major languages of ancient and modern times '. Bibliographical references are appended to the more important articles; most articles are signed with the contributor's initials. For historical surveys of the world's literatures, Shipley directs the user to his companion work, *Encyclopedia of literature* (New York, Philosophical Library, 2 vols, 1946). Help with literary terms will also be found in Meyer Howard Abrams's *A glossary of literary terms* (New York, Holt, 1957), and Karl Beckson and Arthur Ganz's *A reader's guide to literary terms* (London, Thames & Hudson, 1961).

An encyclopedic work limited to one form only is Stephen Spender and Donald Hall's *The concise encyclopedia of English and American poets and poetry* (London, Hutchinson, 2nd ed, 1970), which contains two sorts of articles: those dealing with general topics, and those dealing with particular poets. The general articles, of which there is a separate contents list, include treatments of Australian, Canadian, and other Commonwealth poetry. The articles on individual poets present a minimum of biographical material, being mainly concerned with assessing the poet's achievement according to ' the best contemporary critical opinion ' and in quoting examples of his work. There is a list of contributors (many of them eminent), a bibliography for further reading, an index of poets quoted, and a general index. More scholarly in tone is the *Encyclopedia of poetry and poetics* (Princeton, Princeton UP, 1965), edited by Alex Preminger, which contains about 1,000 entries ranging in length from twenty to more than 20,000 words dealing with the history, theory, technique and criticism of poetry from the earliest times to the present.

Another encyclopedic work concerned with a particular form is *The Oxford companion to the theatre,* edited by Phyllis Hartnoll (London, Oxford UP, 3rd ed, 1967). Though covering ' the theatre in all ages and in all countries ', its aim is to treat what is likely to be of most interest to ' the English-speaking reader '. Its emphasis is on the popular rather than on the literary, and we are told that more will be found on melodrama and music-hall than on comedy and tragedy, and more on actors than on dramatists.

The best-known encyclopedic work dealing with American literature is *The Oxford companion to American literature,* edited by James D Hart (New York, Oxford UP, 4th ed, 1965). This does not confine itself to *belles-lettres* only, and contains short biographies and bibliographies of a host of American authors, with in addition nearly nine hundred summaries and descriptions of important works of literature in all forms. Also included is information on literary schools and movements, literary societies, magazines, anthologies, literary awards, book-collectors, and printers. Canadian literature is taken as part of its coverage. *The reader's encyclopedia of American literature,* edited by Max Herzberg (London, Methuen, 1963), is an illustrated work, again covering Canadian as well as American literature, with entries not only for writers, but also for many individual works, groups and movements, periodicals, and places of literary interest. Norah Story's *The Oxford companion to Canadian history and literature* (Toronto, Oxford UP, 1967) deals with Canadian literature in its broadest sense, its approach to historical and literary materials being an interdependent one.

In a sense, all the works in a collection of literature in English which are not actual literary texts are reference works: bibliographies, catalogues, literary histories and biographies, dictionaries, anthologies. These have been or will be treated in the appropriate chapters of this text book. But to conclude this chapter which began with encyclopedias, there follows a miscellaneous group, related to encyclopedias, comprising a chronological guide to English literature, three dictionaries of proverbs, and several dictionaries of quotations, with a note on concordances.

CHRONOLOGICAL GUIDE

C Ghosh and E G Withycombe's *Annals of English literature, 1475-1950* (Oxford, Clarendon P, 2nd ed, 1961) is a hybrid. On the one hand, it may be regarded as a bibliography, since, as its subtitle states, it lists ' the principal publications of each year together with an alphabetical index of authors with their works '; but on the other hand, its intention, stated in the preface, ' to give the student, at a glance, the main literary output of any year or series of years ', indicates the kind of approach that is typical of an encyclopedia. For example, under the year 1835, there is an alphabetical list of publications by author, starting with Beckford's *Recollections of an excursion to the monasteries of Alcobaça and Batalha,* and concluding with Wordsworth's *Guide through the Lakes,* while notes in the right-hand margin remind us that Mark Twain was born in this year, and also that this was the year of Vigny's drama, *Chatterton.* The compilers, as though pointing up the book's value as a reference guide rather than as a formal bibliography, remind the user that this is ' an elementary manual ', which, while including all the books (but not occasional writings or contributions to periodicals) of the major authors, mentions only a ' selection of the more influential publications of the minors '. American and Commonwealth writers are also featured.

Proverbs were once much more popular than they are nowadays, and they have a considerable importance in English studies, particularly of our earlier literature. A major compilation in this field is Morris Palmer Tilley's *A dictionary of the proverbs in England in the sixteenth and seventeenth centuries* (Ann Arbor, Michigan UP, 1950). In plan, Tilley aims to cover the whole range of Elizabethan drama, supplemented from the Elizabethan proverb collections. His work has an especial value in the study of Shakespeare, in whose day proverbs were at the height of their popularity. The proverbs are arranged by their significant word, and numbered. There is an index of these significant words, a Shakespeare index, and a massive bibliography of sources. Another well-known work on proverbs is *The Oxford dictionary of English proverbs* (Oxford, Clarendon P, 3rd ed, 1970), edited by F P Wilson. Here, the proverbs are arranged, not under their key word, but in alphabetical order by their first word, though variants of what is basically the same proverb are grouped together. Appended to each proverb are illustrative quotations, in chronological order. There is an index of main words which also includes subject entries. For American proverbs there is Archer Taylor and Bartlett Jere Whiting's *A dictionary of American proverbs and proverbial phrases, 1820-1880* (Cambridge, Mass, Belknap P, Harvard UP, 1958); this is alphabetically arranged by key word, and the proverbs are illustrated with many examples from American literature.

In the course of his work a librarian is frequently asked to help to identify literary quotations, and in any English collection it is necessary to have a good selection of dictionaries of quotations. As elsewhere in the field of reference works, the more he has the better.

Experience in reference service invariably demonstrates that every book has its day.

The best dictionary of quotations is *The Oxford dictionary of quotations* (London, Oxford UP, 2nd ed, 1953). It is arranged alphabetically by author, and has a very full index. Reference is given to the source of each quotation. A contrasting arrangement to that of the *Oxford dictionary* is offered by B E Stevenson's *The home book of quotations* (New York, Dodd Mead, 10th ed, 1967), where the quotations are grouped by subject. Again there is a full index, and because of its arrangement, an author index also. Third in importance in this field is John Bartlett's *Familiar quotations* (London, Macmillan, 14th ed, 1969), in which authors are arranged chronologically; it has the essential full index and precise references to sources, and in addition, helpful footnotes where similar phrases have been used by different authors. In origin this is an American work and consequently American authors are given very full coverage. Sir W G Benham's *Book of quotations* (London, Harrap, 1958; first published 1907) arranges its contents in groups: British and American authors, Bible, Greek, Latin, and so on.

Oxford, Stevenson, Bartlett and *Benham* are the best-known, but there are others. Robert Hyman's *The modern dictionary of quotations* (London, Evans, 1962) contains about 25,000 entries (as opposed, for example, to Stevenson's 70,000), arranged by author and indexed by key words. *The Penguin dictionary of quotations,* compiled by J M and M J Cohen (London, Cape, 1962) is similarly arranged and equally hospitable to contemporary quotations. *Everyman's dictionary of quotations and proverbs,* compiled by D C Browning (London, Dent, 1951), has in the region of 10,000 quotations, again arranged alphabetically by author and indexed by key words.

CONCORDANCES

Compilers of dictionaries of quotations have remarked on the provenance of literary quotations: Shakespeare always heads the list, with the *Bible* a close second. They have also observed that some eminent authors, D H Lawrence for example, have never written a quotable or memorable phrase, at least not in the popular sense. For authors such as Shakespeare, or Milton, or Wordsworth, individual concordances exist. Mention of a concordance to an author is always made in the *Concise Cambridge bibliography of English literature;* and A J Walford's *Guide to reference material* also notes them. John Bartlett, mentioned earlier, produced the most comprehensive Shakespeare concordance, for example; Milton has been concordanced by J Bradshaw (1894); and Wordsworth by L Cooper (1911). It is a gratifying thought that the production of a concordance, one of the most laborious of tasks, is particularly amenable to computerization.

CHAPTER VII

Dictionaries and language

DICTIONARIES: ' Dictionaries,' remarked Johnson, ' are like watches; the worst is better than none, and the best cannot be expected to go quite true '. The necessity for dictionaries in an English collection, since they are the keys to the language in which our literature is written, is not a point which needs to be laboured; but for Johnson's ' the best cannot be expected to go quite true ' we may substitute as a second point, that what we must know is not so much which dictionary is the best, but which, for a particular purpose, is the most appropriate. There was an article recently in a British local newspaper in which a journalist was complaining that the *Oxford English dictionary* did not contain all the words and definitions he required in his daily work: his mistake, obvious to any librarian, was in using an ' academy ' dictionary, a dictionary whose value lies in its historical method, when an all-purpose dictionary such as, for example, Webster's, was what he needed.

The honour of being the first known English dictionary belongs to Robert Cawdrey's *A table alphabeticall,* published in 1604. The history of this, and of subsequent dictionaries until the time of Johnson, is traced in *The English dictionary from Cawdrey to Johnson, 1604-1755,* by De Witt T Starnes and Gertrude E Noyes (Chapel Hill, North Carolina UP, 1946), which gives full information about the ' dictionaries, expositors, and glossographies ' printed between those dates and provides ' an exhaustive account of the growth of English lexicography '. A rudimentary survey of dictionaries generally is given by Kenneth Whittaker in his *Dictionaries* (London, Bingley, 1966).

The great landmark in the history of the English dictionary was, of course, the appearance in 1755, in two volumes, of Dr Johnson's *Dictionary.* As the article in the *Encyclopaedia Britannica* by S C Roberts records: ' Johnson's *Dictionary* was hailed with an enthusiasm such as no similar work has ever excited. It was indeed the first dictionary which could be read with pleasure. The definitions show so much acuteness of thought and command of language, and the passages quoted from poets, divines and philosophers are so skilfully selected, that a leisure hour may always be very agreeably spent in turning over the pages. The faults of the book resolve themselves, for the most part, into one great fault. Johnson was a wretched etymologist.' Roberts does not mention in this passage another pleasure of Johnson's *Dictionary*: its humour. Of his own calling, Johnson supplies this definition: ' Lexicographer. A writer of dictionaries; a harmless drudge.'

No fewer than thirteen hundred 'harmless drudges' were occupied in producing the greatest of all dictionaries, *A new English dictionary on historical principles*, edited by Sir J A H Murray and others (Oxford, Clarendon P, 10 vols, 1888-1928), reissued in 1933 (12 vols and supplement) as the *Oxford English dictionary,* and hence referred to as Murray's or the *NED* or the *OED*. The aim, first proposed in 1857 by the Philological Society, was to produce ' a dictionary which, by the completeness of its vocabulary, and by the application of the historical method to the life and use of words, might be worthy of the English language and of English scholarship '. There is no debate but that this aim was realised. Its first volume notes that the thirteen hundred contributors selected millions of quotations from more than five thousand authors of all periods, and the result is a dictionary of nearly half a million words illustrated by one and a half million quotations. Taking as its field ' English words now in general use ', it sets out:

' 1) to show, with regard to each individual word, when, how, in what shape, and with what signification, it became English; what development of form and meaning it has since received; which of its uses have, in the course of time, become obsolete, and which still survive; what new uses have since arisen, by what processes, and when:

' 2) to illustrate these facts by a series of quotations ranging from the first known occurrence of the word to the latest, or down to the present day; the word being thus made to exhibit its own history and meaning: and

' 3) to treat the etymology of each word strictly on the basis of historical fact, and in accordance with the methods and results of modern philological science.'

67

A descendant of this monumental work is the *Shorter Oxford English dictionary* (3rd ed rev, 1964), which aims 'to present in miniature all the features of the principal work', a 'quintessence' of its 'vast materials'. It is about one sixth the length of the *OED*, and this has been achieved mainly by reducing the number of illustrative quotations and by shortening the etymologies: two thirds of the original's words are retained, supplemented by 'such technical and scientific terms as are most frequently met with'. Its *Preface* describes its character as still being a 'historical dictionary of English', that is, still concentrating on giving for each word 'the chronological sequence in the development of meaning'.

Quite different in character, though the same medium size, is Webster's *Third new international dictionary of the English language* (London, Bell, 1962), which has altogether a much longer history: this is the eighth of a series which began in 1828. Its primary objective is 'precise, sharp defining', and it is extremely wide-ranging and well-balanced. Among its editors, states the *Preface,* are 'a mathematician, a physicist, a chemist, a botanist, a biologist, a philosopher, a political scientist, a comparative religionist, a classicist, a historian, and a librarian as well as philologists, linguists, etymologists, and phoneticians whose specialty is the English language itself'. It excludes words which had become obsolete before 1755.

A specific example may serve to demonstrate how, even though the *Shorter Oxford* and *Webster's* are both excellent dictionaries, one can be more appropriate than the other in a particular instance. The word 'shambles' is most frequently used nowadays to describe a mess or muddle. But if you check its meaning in the *Shorter Oxford* all you will find is its correct, original meaning: a place where meat is sold, a slaughterhouse, a place of carnage or wholesale slaughter. In *Webster's,* however, you will find it also defined as a scene of great disorder, and great confusion, the first definition even being illustrated by a quotation from S J Perelman.

The two best desk dictionaries are first, again of the *Oxford* line, the *Concise Oxford dictionary of current English* (5th ed, 1964), described by Whittaker as 'a top rate no nonsense dictionary'; and second, *Chambers's twentieth century dictionary* (Edinburgh, 1959), which is surprisingly comprehensive with entries for about 150,000 words.

Dictionaries are important for any period of the English language; it is a very natural trap to assume that an eighteenth-century writer is using a word to mean what that word means today. What is more apparent, however, is the need for a dictionary when dealing with the unfamiliar language of the Anglo-Saxon or Middle English periods. For Anglo-Saxon, there is J Bosworth's *An Anglo-Saxon dictionary*, edited and supplemented by T N Toller (Oxford, Clarendon P, 1882-98; 1908-21), noted by Walford as being the 'only full-scale work generally available'; and John R Clark Hall's *A concise dictionary of Anglo-Saxon* (Cambridge, Cambridge UP, 4th ed, 1960), which is more suitable for the student than for the specialist. For the Middle English period, Francis Henry Stratmann and Henry Bradley's *A Middle-English dictionary* (London, Oxford UP, 1891) is the most comprehensive dictionary in completed form, and gives etymologies, meanings and citations from the works of individual authors for about 17,000 words; while H Kurath and S H Kuhn's *Middle English dictionary* (Ann Arbor, Michigan UP, 1952-) is still appearing in parts.

American English also requires the use of a dictionary. The two famous works here are Sir William Craigie and James R Hulbert's *A dictionary of American English on historical principles* (London, Oxford UP, 4 vols, 1938-44), modelled on the *OED*; and Mitford M Mathew's *A dictionary of Americanisms on historical principles* (London, Oxford UP, 1951), which is limited to words and expressions which originated in America.

Scots words are also well-served; first, by *The Scottish national dictionary*, edited by William Grant and David D Murison (Edinburgh, Scottish National Dictionary Association, 1931-), dealing with Scottish words in use since c1700; and second, by Sir William Craigie's *A dictionary of the older Scottish tongue* (London, Oxford UP, 1931-), which is concerned with the period from the twelfth century to the end of the seventeenth. These two dictionaries are still in progress; a concise completed work is *Chambers's Scots dictionary*, compiled by A Warrack (Edinburgh, Chambers, 1911).

Regional variations of English are in as much need of explanation as national variations. Joseph Wright's *The English dialect diction-*

ary (London, Frowde, 6 vols, 1898-1905), despite its title, deals with the dialects of Scotland, Wales and Ireland as well as with those of England. This is a great work compiled by a remarkable man; it defines more than 100,000 dialect words, giving the regions where each word is found, along with pronunciation, etymology and illustrative quotations. Currently in course of publication is Harold Orton and Eugen Dieth's *Survey of English dialects* (published for the University of Leeds by E J Arnold, Leeds, 1962-), which is making public the survey of English dialects carried out between the years 1950 and 1961 by the English Department at Leeds and whose ultimate aim is the compilation of a linguistic atlas of England.

Another variation of English is slang. Best-known for lexicographical work in this field is Eric Partridge, whose *A dictionary of slang and unconventional English* (London, Routledge, 6th ed, 2 vols, 1967) is a very respectable treatment of what is a not quite respectable subject. The first of his two volumes is basically the original 1937 edition of the *Dictionary,* the second being supplementary material accumulated since then. Partridge treats his material historically, giving origin, date and source as well as definition. The American equivalent is H Wentworth and S B Flexner's *Dictionary of American slang* (London, Harrap, new ed, 1967), which also gives the source and date of its entries in their various meanings. Partridge has also produced *A dictionary of the underworld, British and American* (London, Routledge, 3rd ed, 1968).

All these dictionaries dealing with the English language, in its standard form, and in its period, national, regional and even class variations, are concerned primarily with definition. Concentrating on the etymological aspect only, there is Walter W Skeat's *An etymological dictionary of the English language* (Oxford, Clarendon P, 4th ed, 1910); there is also now *The Oxford dictionary of English etymology,* edited by Charles Talbot Onions (Oxford, Clarendon P, 1966); and on simpler lines for the general reader, Ernest Weekley's *An etymological dictionary of modern English* (London, Murray, 1921) and Partridge's *Origins: a short etymological dictionary of modern English* (London, Routledge, 4th ed, 1966). Concentrating on pronunciation only, is Daniel Jones's *Everyman's English pronouncing dictionary* (London, Dent, 13th ed, 1967).

Specialization in dictionaries does not stop here. Within English vocabulary itself there are categories of words and phrases—synonyms, idioms, clichés—which have been separately treated in dictionaries. An outstanding and famous example is P M Roget's *Thesaurus of English words and phrases* (London, Longmans, rev ed, 1962), which is composed of lists of similar and contrasted words classified according to the ideas they express. For example, if you look up the word ' thief ', you will read : ' thieving fraternity, swell mob, light-fingered gentry, den of thieves . . . crook . . . stealer, lifter, filcher, purloiner, pilferer, snapper-up of unconsidered trifles; sneaker, sneak-thief, shop-lifter; pick-pocket, swell mobsman, cut-purse, purse-snatcher, bag-snatcher . . .' and so on for half a page. A full index complements this classified arrangement. Another comprehensive dictionary of synonyms is *Webster's new dictionary of synonyms* (Springfield, Mass, Merriam, 1968), whose sub-title describes its aims concisely : ' a dictionary of discriminated synonyms and antonyms and analogous and contrasted words '. Quotations are use to illustrate use. Idioms and clichés constitute a further important feature of the English language. Three volumes compiled by V H Collins, *A book of English idioms* (London, Longmans, 1956), *A second book of English idioms* (1958), and *A third book of English idioms* (1960), each contain about one thousand idiomatic phrases arranged alphabetically by key word, and defined. Eric Partridge's *A dictionary of clichés* (London, Routledge, 4th ed, 1950) is concerned with the same area, but whereas an ' idiom ' is to be respected, a ' cliché ' is to be avoided. Guidance on usage generally is to be found in H W Fowler's *A dictionary of modern English usage* (Oxford, Clarendon P, 2nd ed, 1965), where a series of alphabetically-arranged articles advise the reader on such thorny matters as the correct use of, for example, ' due to ' as opposed to ' owing to '. Recently published was Wilson Follett's *Modern American usage: a guide* (London, Longmans, 1966), edited and completed by Jacques Barzun.

LANGUAGE : BIBLIOGRAPHIES

Dictionaries are treated, as in all other material on the English language, in Arthur G Kennedy's *A bibliography of writings on the English language, from the beginning of printing to the end of 1922*

(Cambridge, Mass, Harvard UP, 1927), the intention of which is to provide 'exhaustive information', the *Preface* claiming that 'for the period from 1875 to 1922 it is not likely that much of importance has been overlooked'. The material is arranged in ten chapters : General collections; General and historical writings; English paleography; English and other languages; Anglo-Saxon or Old English (to about AD 1100); Middle English (to about 1500 AD); Modern English; Recent tendencies in English; History of the study of the English language; Theory and method of the study and teaching of English.

Within each chapter, the material is again grouped, this time into three categories: general books and articles, books and articles on general topics, books and articles on special topics. Under each topical sub-division, arrangement is chronological. All the items are numbered, and some idea of the size of this bibliography may be gauged from the fact that the last entry is 13,402. There is, finally, an index of authors and reviewers, and an index of subjects.

Another language bibliography is R C Alston's *A bibliography of the English language from the invention of printing to the year 1800: a systematic record of writings on English, and on other languages in English, based on the collections of the principal libraries of the world* (printed for the author by E J Arnold, Leeds, 1965-), a heroic one-man effort belonging in spirit to an earlier age of monumental works: 'I have, at all times, been responsible, unaided for the basic research, correspondence, checking and typing'. Beginning as a collection of notes on early printed material relating to the history of the English language, 'with a view to publishing a supplement to the late Arthur G Kennedy's *Bibliography of writings on the English language*', it swelled to twenty volumes, based on files containing over 25,000 entries with locations in 800 libraries throughout the world. Alston decided to abandon the idea of producing a supplement to Kennedy, but instead to offer a 'completely fresh work, in which attention to bibliographical detail, and a personal scrutiny of every item would constitute inviolable principles'. The twenty volumes, which are not appearing in strict sequence, are planned to be as follows:

I English grammars written in English

II English grammars written in other languages: polyglot grammars and dictionaries

III Miscellaneous works dealing with various aspects of English: grammar, non-technical glossaries, theory of grammar

IV Spelling

V The English dictionary

VI Rhetoric: prosody: rhyme: pronunciation: elocution: phonetics

VII Logic: philosophy: epistemology: universal language

VIII Short-hand

IX Non-standard English: cant: dialect

X Education: teaching of languages: surdo-mutism

XI Place and personal names: geographical dictionaries, glossaries: gazetteers: London street names, etc

XII Romance languages (grammars, dictionaries, glossaries, spelling, pronunciation)

XIII Germanic languages (grammars, dictionaries, glossaries, spelling, pronunciation)

XIV Other languages (grammars, dictionaries, etc)

XV Latin language (1500-1650)

XVI Latin language (1651-1800): Greek language

XVII Vocabulary of science, technology, arts, crafts, sports, pastimes

XVIII Periodical literature: essay material (all subjects)

XIX Material in manuscript

XX Indexes.

For each item he describes, Alston gives abbreviated details of the title-page, pagination, references to standard bibliographies and catalogues, locations in libraries, references to secondary material (articles, monographs, essays), references to contemporary reviews and a brief mention of the principal contents. The items are numbered, and arranged chronologically. It will be seen that the main emphasis of the work is on the ' bibliographical detail '.

Two more specialized bibliographies are G Scheurweghs's *Analytical bibliography of writings on modern English morphology and syntax, 1877-1960* (University of Louvain, 4 vols, 1963-68); and Richard W Bailey and Dolores M Burton's *English stylistics: a bibliography* (Cambridge, Mass, MIT Press, 1968). The first of these deals with both periodical and monograph literature; and the subject of the second is defined by its compilers as 'the literary uses of language qua language '.

LANGUAGE : GENERAL STUDIES, GRAMMAR, ETC
The earlier part of this chapter dealt with dictionaries, but of course, provision of material on the English language goes beyond just dictionaries. The Kennedy bibliography will give some idea of the full range. In even the most modest collection of literature in English the librarian should provide one or two shelves of books on the language. The best-known general studies are Henry Bradley's *The making of English* (1904); Albert C Baugh's *A history of the English language* (2nd ed, 1957); Otto Jespersen's *Growth and structure of the English language* (9th ed, 1968); Henry C Wyld's *The historical study of mother tongue* (1906), *The growth of English* (1907) and *A short history of English* (1927); Logan Pearsall Smith's *The English language* (3rd ed, 1966); and C L Wrenn's *The English language* (1952). On pronunciation and phonetics, there are Daniel Jones's *The pronunciation of English* (4th ed, 1956) and *An outline of English phonetics* (10th ed, 1964); and Ida C Ward's *The phonetics of English* (4th ed, 1945). On etymology, there is Walter W Skeat's *Principles of English etymology* (2 series, 1878-91). The standard full-scale grammar is Otto Jespersen's *A modern English grammar on historical principles* (7 vols, 1909-49); the same scholar produced a shorter work, *The essentials of English grammar* (1933). American English is surveyed historically in H L Mencken's *The American language* (4th ed, 3 vols, 1936-48). Indispensable for all aspects of the study of Australian and New Zealand vocabulary are E E Morris's *Austral English* (1898), and S J Baker's *The Australian language* (2nd ed, 1966).

In an English collection there is also a need for some guidance on the actual writing of English. The most refreshing of recent books on this topic was Sir Ernest Gowers's *Plain words* (1948), which has since become *The complete plain words* (1957). Two simpler works are G H Vallins's *Good English* (1952) and *Better English* (1955). And a stand-by for many years has been H W and F G Fowler's *The King's English* (3rd ed, 1931).

74

CHAPTER VIII

Anthologies and collections

THE VERY NUMBER of anthologies available bears witness to the usefulness and popularity of this type of work. To have literary texts from many sources brought together in one volume is an obvious convenience, both from the point of view of compactness and from the point of view of economy. But there is a great deal more to it than that. In many instances, the texts in an anthology are just not readily available in any other form. Also, the actual contribution of the editor of a good anthology is considerable: first, we benefit from his taste and scholarship in that his selection is less random and more informed than ours could be; second, he takes care to offer authoritative versions of the texts he is anthologizing; and third, very often he supplies an introduction, notes, and other critical apparatus. Collections share all of these advantages, on a larger scale.

Because anthologies are so numerous, lists of them are essential. The *Concise Cambridge bibliography* is excellent in this respect, indicating the appropriate anthologies for each period on a scale which is very liberal considering the overall size of that volume; no anthology of real importance is omitted. Very useful also, is F Seymour Smith's *An English library,* especially since he uses asterisks to pick out those to be particularly recommended. *The reader's adviser: a guide to the best in literature* (11th ed, by Winifred F Courtney, vol 1, New York, Bowker, 1968) contains very full lists of anthologies, grouped by the form—verse, drama, prose —anthologized. F W Bateson's *Guide to English literature* is helpful in a different way: since the character of this book is highly evaluative, his comments on various anthologies are illuminating. Spender and Hall's *Concise encyclopedia of English and American poets and poetry,* in its section on further reading, is surprisingly comprehensive in its coverage of verse anthologies. Finally, it is worth noting that anthologies are one of the few categories of material omitted by Walford in his *Guide to reference material.*

Anthologies are best surveyed by form, because this is usually the basis of their compilation, but a few comments are called for on general and period anthologies and collections.

A completely general anthology is George Bagshawe Harrison's *Major British writers* (New York, Harcourt, 2 vols, 1959), particularly commended by Bateson for the eminence of its team of editors, its notes, and its introductions. The twenty two authors anthologized include Chaucer, Spenser, Shakespeare, Bacon, Donne, Milton, Swift, Pope, Johnson and Boswell, Wordsworth, Keats, Browning, Arnold, Shaw, Yeats, and Eliot.

A general collection, not limited to any form or any period, but using rarity as its main criterion, is Liverpool University's *Liverpool reprints,* the first of which appeared in 1948; the name of the series was changed in 1956, with the appearance of the twelfth reprint, to *English reprints.* The aim is to provide inexpensive texts of works which would be otherwise very difficult to obtain.

PERIOD

When we come to period collections, the outstanding example is that put out by the Early English Text Society, comprising two long series, the Original Series and the Extra Series. The society was founded in 1864 by Frederick James Furnivall 'to bring the mass of unprinted Early English literature within the reach of students'. This collection, published by the Oxford University Press, is an automatic purchase for university and reference libraries. Also for this early period of English literature, are the following standard anthologies: W J Sedgefield's *An Anglo-Saxon book of verse and prose* (Manchester, Manchester UP, 1928), which is a combination of the same author's *An Anglo-Saxon verse book* (1922) and *An Anglo-Saxon prose book* (1928); Bruce Dickins and R M Wilson's *Early Middle English texts* (London, Bowes, 1951) covers the twelfth and thirteenth centuries, as does J A W Bennett and G V Smithers's *Early Middle English verse and prose* (Oxford, Clarendon P, 2nd ed, 1968); and Kenneth Sisam's *Fourteenth-century verse and prose* (Oxford, Clarendon P, 1921).

For the seventeenth century, a highly-praised period anthology is that edited by Helen Constance White, Ruth C Wallerstein and Ricardo Quintana: *Seventeenth-century verse and prose* (New York, Macmillan, 2 vols, 1951). The eighteenth century has its own collection: the publications of the Augustan Reprint Society, which produces facsimiles of items difficult to obtain. The first publication of the society appeared in 1946.

However, as remarked earlier, anthologies are usually linked to a particular form, and of course, the form most anthologized is poetry. After all, the most famous of all anthologies is probably Francis Turner Palgrave's *The golden treasury of the best songs and lyrical poems in the English language,* which first appeared in 1861, and which is now available from Oxford UP, or Macmillan, or Collins, or Everyman. Next to it on the shelves of any library will stand the best one-volume anthology of poetry that there is, Sir Arthur Quiller-Couch's *The Oxford book of English verse, 1250-1918* (London, Oxford UP, new ed, 1939). Other notable general anthologies of English poetry are: W H Auden and Norman Pearson's *Poets of the English language* (London, Eyre & Spottiswoode, 5 vols, 1952), a comprehensive anthology with notes and biographies; Cleanth Brooks and Robert Penn Warren's *Understanding poetry* (New York, Holt, 3rd ed, 1960), which contains critical analyses; John Hayward's *The Faber book of English verse* (London, Faber, 1958), described by Bateson as 'a first-rate selection'; Edith Sitwell's *The Atlantic book of British and American poetry* (London, Gollancz, 2 vols, 1959), a highly personal selection by an eminent poet, with critical prefaces; W H Auden and John Garrett's *The poet's tongue* (London, Bell, 1935), which places its emphasis on ballads and lighter verse; Denys Kilham Roberts's *The centuries poetry* (Harmondsworth, Penguin, 5 vols, 1938-53), which ranges in its first volume from Chaucer to Shakespeare, in its second from Donne to Dryden, in its third from Pope to Keats, in its fourth from Hood to Hardy, and in its fifth from Bridges to the present day; Ronald and Margaret Bottrall's *Collected English verse* (London, Sidgwick & Jackson, 1947); Bonamy Dobrée and Sir Herbert Read's *The London book of English verse* (London, Eyre & Spottiswoode, 3rd ed, 1956), in which the material is arranged

77

into kinds—for example, narrative verse; and William Peacock's *English verse* (World's Classics, Oxford UP, 5 vols, 1928-31).

Period anthologies of poetry are equally numerous. For the earliest period, the most important anthology is George P Krapp and Elliott van K Dobbie's *The Anglo-Saxon poetic records* (New York, Columbia UP, 6 vols, 1931-53). Others are: Charles W Kennedy's *An anthology of Old English poetry* (New York, Oxford UP, 1960) and *Early English Christian poetry translated into alliterative verse* (New York, Oxford UP, 1952); and R K Gordon's selected and translated *Anglo-Saxon poetry* (Everyman, London, Dent, 1954).

The 'best general selection of fifteenth- and early sixteenth-century poetry' in Bateson's opinion is Eleanor Prescott Hammond's *English verse between Chaucer and Surrey* (Durham, NC, Duke UP, 1927). Two scholars well-known for their work on this Middle English period are Carleton Brown and Rossell Hope Robbins; Brown has compiled *English lyrics of the XIIIth century* (Oxford UP, 1932). *Religious lyrics of the XIVth century* (Oxford UP, 1924), and *Religious lyrics of the XVth century* (Oxford UP, 1939); Robbins has compiled *Secular lyrics of the XIVth and XVth centuries* (Oxford UP, 1952) and *Historical poems of the XIVth and XVth centuries* (New York, Columbia UP, 1959). Celia and Kenneth Sisam have recently compiled *The Oxford book of medieval verse* (Oxford, Clarendon P, 1970), which covers the whole range of verse forms. Also useful, are Sir E K Chambers and F Sidgwick's *Early English lyrics* (1907); Reginald Thorne Davies's *Medieval English lyrics* (1963); and George Leslie Brook's *The Harley lyrics* (Manchester, Manchester UP, 3rd ed, 1964). For the romances there is Walter Hoyt French and Charles Brockway Hale's *Middle English metrical romances* (New York, Prentice-Hall, 1930); and for another important form of Middle English poetry, Richard Leighton Greene's *The Early English carols* (1935).

John William Hebel and Hoyt Hopewell Hudson's *Poetry of the English renaissance, 1509-1660* (New York, Crofts, 1929) bridges the next period. Collections of Elizabethan poetry began in Elizabethan times, with *Tottel's miscellany* (1557) containing the sonnets of Wyatt and Surrey, and *Englands Helicon* (1600). Modern anthologies include: Sir E K Chambers's *The Oxford book of sixteenth century verse* (Oxford UP, 1932); Norman E McClure's *Sixteenth century English poetry* (New York, Harper, 1954); Gerald Bullett's *Silver poets of the sixteenth century* (Everyman, 1947)—Wyatt, Surrey, Sidney, Raleigh, Sir John Davies; and Norman Ault's *Elizabethan lyrics from the original texts* (London, Longmans, 1925). Norman Ault has also compiled, for the next period, *Seventeenth-century lyrics from the original texts* (Longmans, 1928). For the same period, there is Sir Herbert Grierson and Geoffrey Bullough's *The Oxford book of seventeenth century verse* (1934), and the following: Robert Cecil Bald's *Seventeenth-century English poetry* (New York, Harper, 1959); Robert Guy Howarth's *Minor poets of the seventeenth century* (Everyman, 1953)—Carew, Herbert of Cherbury, Lovelace, Suckling; George Saintsbury's *Minor poets of the Caroline period* (Oxford UP, 3 vols, 1905-21); Sir Herbert Grierson's *Metaphysical lyrics and poems* (Oxford UP, 1921); and again on the metaphysicals, Helen Gardner's *The metaphysical poets* (Oxford UP, 1961). Covering satire on public affairs—the dominant poetic genre in the fifty four years between the Restoration and the death of Queen Anne—is *Poems on affairs of state: Augustan satirical verse, 1660-1714* (New Haven, Yale UP, 1963-); published so far are vol 1, 1660-1678, ed by G de F Lord; vol 2, 1678-1681, ed by E F Mengel; vol 3, 1682-1685, ed by H H Schless; vol 4, 1685-1688, ed by G M Crump; and vol 6, 1697-1704, ed by F H Ellis.

For the eighteenth century, there is first, an older anthology, characterized by Bateson as 'indispensable': this is Alexander Chalmers's *The works of the English poets from Chaucer to Cowper* (21 vols, 1810). More familiar, more accessible, and very highly regarded, is Ronald S Crane's *A collection of English poems, 1660-1800* (New York, Harper, 1932); as is also David Nichol Smith's *The Oxford book of eighteenth century verse* (1926). Less general collections of eighteenth century poetry are: Hugh I'Anson Fausset's *Minor poets of the eighteenth century* (Everyman, 1930), a substantially complete edition of five poets; Kathleen W Campbell's *Poems on several occasions written in the eighteenth century* (Oxford, Blackwell, 1926); Iolo A Williams's *The shorter poems of the eighteenth century* (London, Heinemann, 1923); and Donald Davie's *The late Augustans* (London, Heinemann, 1958), containing only the longer poems.

For the nineteenth century, another older work is still useful. This is Alfred Henry Miles's *The poets and the poetry of the century* (London, Hutchinson, 10 vols, 1891-7), which has biographical notes and critical essays; its strong point is the number of poets included. Dedicated to Miles is George MacBeth's recent *The Penguin book of Victorian verse* (Harmondsworth, 1969); and that very skilful anthologist, John Hayward, has compiled two volumes covering this period: *The Oxford book of nineteenth century verse* (1964), and *Nineteenth century poetry* (London, Chatto, 1932). Also in the *Oxford* series, are Sir Humphrey Milford's *The Oxford book of English verse of the Romantic period, 1798-1887* (1935), and Sir Arthur Quiller-Couch's *The Oxford book of Victorian verse* (1912).

Bridging into the modern period is that series of volumes issued by the Poetry Bookshop, London, from 1913 to 1922: *Georgian poetry, 1911-22*. One of the earlier anthologies of modern verse was compiled by W B Yeats: *The Oxford book of modern verse* (1936). More recent outstanding anthologies have been: Michael Roberts's *The Faber book of modern verse* (1951); John Heath-Stubbs and David Wright's *The Faber book of twentieth century verse* (1953); C Day Lewis and John Lehmann's *The Chatto book of modern poetry, 1915-51* (1956); and Lord David Cecil and Allen Tate's *Modern verse in English, 1900-1950* (London, Eyre & Spottiswoode, 1958). Also since 1952, there has been the PEN annual, *New poems*.

Quite apart from general and period anthologies of poetry, there are anthologies devoted to particular types of poetry or particular themes in poetry. Ballads, for example, have been well collected and well anthologized. The greatest and most exhaustive collection of ballads was that made by Francis J Child, *English and Scottish popular ballads* (Oxford UP, reissued, 3 vols, 1957). Other collections are: James Kinsley's new edition of *The Oxford book of ballads* (1969); Hyder Edward Rollins's *A Pepysian garland* (Cambridge, Cambridge UP, 1922), which contains ballads of the period 1595-1639, and the same compiler's larger collections for the period 1535-1702, *The Pepys ballads* (Oxford UP, 8 vols, 1929-32); and on a more modest scale, V de Sola Pinto and A E Rodway's *The common muse: an anthology of popular British ballad poetry, XVth-*

XXth century (London, Chatto, 1957), which includes printed street ballads.

Turning to another type of poetry, there are two *Oxford* volumes of religious verse: Lord David Cecil's *The Oxford book of Christian verse* (1940); and David H S Nicholson and A H E Lee's *The Oxford book of English mystical verse* (1916), which collects from the thirteenth century onwards.

Poetry of a lighter kind is anthologized in W H Auden's *The Oxford book of light verse* (1938) and Roger Lancelyn Green's *A century of humorous verse, 1850-1950* (Everyman, 1959). Also on a lighter note are: Iona and Peter Opie's *An Oxford dictionary of nursery rhymes* (1951); James Orchard Halliwell's *Popular rhymes and nursery tales of England* (1849; reprinted 1970); R L Greene's *A selection of English carols* (Oxford UP, 1962); Percy Dearmer and others, *The Oxford book of carols* (1928); and Edmund Horace Fellowes's *English madrigal verse, 1588-1632* (3rd ed, by F W Sternfeld and D Greer, 1967).

Ernest Rhys's *The golden treasury of longer poems* (Everyman, 1921) has a self-explanatory title; it ranges in time from Chaucer to de la Mare. De la Mare's name reminds us inevitably of children: children have not been forgotten by the anthologizers. De la Mare himself has compiled *Come hither* (London, Constable, 1923); there are also Pamela Whitlock's *All day long: an anthology of poetry for children* (Oxford UP, 1954) and Janet Adam Smith's *The Faber book of children's verse* (1953).

Poetry has also been anthologized on a national basis. Francis Otto Matthiessen has compiled *The Oxford book of American verse* (1950); A J M Smith, *The Oxford book of Canadian verse* (1960) and *Modern Canadian verse in English and French* (1968); Judith Wright, *A book of Australian verse* (Oxford UP, 1956); Robert Chapman and Jonathan Bennett, *An anthology of New Zealand verse* (Oxford UP, 1956); Vincent O'Sullivan, *An anthology of twentieth-century New Zealand poetry* (Oxford UP, 1970); Walter Murdoch and Alan Mulgan, *A book of Australian and New Zealand verse* (Oxford UP, 1951, based on the now superseded *Oxford book of Australian verse*, 1918); and nearer home, there is John Buchan's *The Northern muse* (London, Nelson, 1924), an anthology of Scots vernacular poetry, complemented by Douglas Young's *Scottish verse, 1851-1951* (Nelson, 1952), and more recently, by *The Oxford book of Scottish verse,* edited by John MacQueen and Tom Scott (Oxford, 1966).

DRAMA

When we come to anthologies and collections of plays, we begin right back in the eighteenth century with Robert Dodsley's *A select collection of old plays* (12 vols, 1744), subsequently edited and enlarged to include eighty three plays, by W Carew Hazlitt (15 vols, 1874-6). Another older work also retains its value: Charles Lamb's *Specimens of English dramatic poets* (1808). Likewise concerned with the early drama, are the publications of the Malone Society, which was founded in 1906 'for the purpose of making accessible materials for the study of the Early English drama', its publications consisting of 'reprints of old plays and of collections containing documents and notes relating to stage history'; and W Bang's *Materialien zur Kunde des älteren englischen Dramas* (Louvain, 1902-).

But while the main interests of Dodsley, Lamb, the Malone Society and Bang are centred around the great period of English drama, that is, the Shakespearean period, anthologies have also been compiled of pre-Shakespearean plays. The greatest of these is Joseph Q Adams's *Chief pre-Shakespearean dramas* (New York, Houghton, 1924), in which, as Bateson notes, 'everything of dramatic interest down to *c* 1570' has been included. The miracle and morality plays which precede the Elizabethan age are anthologized in A W Pollard's *English miracle plays, moralities, and interludes* (Oxford UP, 1927); A C Cawley's *Everyman and medieval miracle plays* (Everyman, 1956); and the famous *York cycle of mystery plays,* edited by J S Purvis (London, SPCK, 1957). Also pre-Shakespearean are the plays in John Matthews Manly's *Specimens of pre-Shakespearean drama* (Boston, Ginn, 2 vols, 1897-8); John William Cunliffe's *Early English classical tragedies* (Oxford UP, 1912); Frederick Samuel Boas's *Five pre-Shakespearean comedies* (Oxford, World's Classics, 1934); and Ashley Horace Thorndike's *Minor Elizabethan drama* (Everyman, 2 vols, 1910), the first volume of which contains pre-Shakespearean tragedies, the second pre-Shakespearean comedies.

82

Returning to the Elizabethans, one of the anthologies most used by university students is C F Tucker Brooke and N B Paradise's *English drama, 1580-1642* (New York, Heath, 1933); and a recently-begun series of distinguished editions of the plays of the period are the *Revels plays* (1958-), edited by Clifford Leech. Some representative comedies have been collected by Archibald Kennedy McIlwraith in *Five Elizabethan comedies* (Oxford, World's Classics, 1934), while for history plays there is William Armstrong's *Elizabethan history plays* (Oxford, World's Classics, 1965). A K McIlwraith has also collected *Five Stuart tragedies* (World's Classics, 1953), which range from *Bussy D'Ambois* (1607) to *'Tis pity she's a whore* (1633). A useful volume of play synopses is Karl J Holzknecht's *Outlines of Tudor and Stuart plays, 1497-1642* (London, Methuen, 1963; first published in America in 1947); apart from synopses, the author also provides short biographical sketches of the playwrights, critical estimates of their work, notes on sources, and bibliographical information about the earliest printed versions, the best single and collected editions, and recent collections of Elizabethan plays in which individual works have been reprinted. Familiar for many years to librarians and students has been *The Mermaid series: the best plays of the old dramatists,* edited by Havelock Ellis, most volumes being devoted to a particular dramatist (among them Marlowe, Massinger, Middleton, Dekker, Shirley, Otway, Ford and Heywood) and containing carefully-edited texts of the plays, with introductions. Since 1964 these have begun to be re-edited by Philip Brockbank and Brian Morris as *The new Mermaids,* each volume containing a single play, with introduction and a select bibliography. The Restoration drama has been anthologized by Bonamy Dobrée: his *Five Restoration tragedies* (World's Classics, 1926) comprises plays by Dryden, Otway, Southerne, Rowe, and Addison; and his *Five heroic plays* (World's Classics, 1960), contains plays performed between 1665 and 1667. *Representative English comedies,* edited by Charles Mills Gayley and others (New York, Macmillan, 4 vols, 1903-36), spans from pre-Shakespearean drama to this period, the period of Dryden.

Eighteenth century drama has been anthologized by John Hampden in *Eighteenth century plays* (Everyman, 1928), and William

Duncan Taylor in *Eighteenth century comedy* (new ed by S Trussler, Oxford UP, 1969).

The nineteenth century was not a great period for drama. However, Michael R Booth has compiled *English plays of the nineteenth century* (Oxford, Clarendon P, 1969-), the first two volumes of which contain examples of tragedy, melodrama, and the ' drama ', whilst further volumes will illustrate comedy, farce, extravaganza, and burlesque. Two minor collections are the World's Classics volumes edited by George Rowell, *Nineteenth century plays* (1953) and *Late Victorian plays, 1890-1914* (1968).

For our own time, one of the worthiest series is *Methuen's modern plays,* which includes works by British playwrights, such as John Arden, Harold Pinter and Brendan Behan, as well as translations from Continental dramatists.

PROSE

Prose anthologies are not as numerous as those for poetry or drama. A general prose anthology published recently is *The Pelican book of English prose,* the first volume of which (1970), edited by Roger Sharrock, covers up to 1780, and the second (1969), edited by Raymond Williams, from 1780 to the present day. Two of the *Oxford books* are devoted to prose: Sir Arthur Quiller-Couch's *The Oxford book of English prose* (1925); and James Sutherland's *The Oxford book of English talk* (1953), which is a widely-gathered collection of recorded conversation from the sixteenth to the present century.

An outstanding collection of fiction is George Saintsbury and Philip Henderson's *Shorter novels* (Everyman, 3 vols, 1920-30), which draws its material from the Elizabethan period, the seventeenth and the eighteenth centuries; while William Harlin McBurney's *Four before Richardson* (Lincoln, University of Nebraska P, 1963) comprises selected English novels, 1720-1727.

Period anthologies of prose include: William Matthews's *Later medieval English prose* (London, Peter Owen, 1962); R W Chambers and Marjorie Daunt's *A book of London English, 1384-1425* (Oxford, Clarendon P, 1931); *Prose of the English renaissance,* edited by John William Hebel and others (New York, Appleton,

84

1952); and John Dover Wilson's *Life in Shakespeare's England: a book of Elizabethan prose* (Cambridge, Cambridge UP, 1911).

LITERARY CRITICISM

A collection of *English literary criticism of the 18th century*, comprising 208 original texts in 225 volumes, with an introduction to the series by René Wellek, is being published (1970-) by the Garland Press, New York. For two earlier periods there are G Gregory Smith's *Elizabethan critical essays* (Oxford, Clarendon P, 2 vols, 1904) and J E Spingarn's *Critical essays of the seventeenth century* (Oxford, Clarendon P, 3 vols, 1908), both highly-respected standard works.

CHAPTER IX

Periodicals

PERIODICALS ARE SO actual, so of the present, that it is quite easy to overlook the fact that they have a long history. Familiar even now are the *Tatler* and the *Spectator,* which began early in the eighteenth century. Later, came the *Gentleman's magazine* (1731); and in the first half of the nineteenth century, the *Edinburgh review* (1802), the *Quarterly review* (1809), and *Blackwood's magazine* (1817). Then came the *Fortnightly review* (1865), the *Contemporary review* (1866), and *Nineteenth century* (1877). The very beginning of the twentieth century saw the birth (1902) of the *Times literary supplement.*

Walter James Graham has written two books on the history of the periodical: *The beginnings of English literary periodicals* (New York, Oxford UP, 1926), which brings the story down to Addison and Steele; and *English literary periodicals* (New York, Nelson, 1930). *Studies in the early English periodical,* edited by Richmond P Bond (Chapel Hill, North Carolina UP, 1957), deals with the years 1700-1760; while Robert Donald Spector's *English literary periodicals and the climate of opinion during the Seven Years' War* (The Hague, Mouton, 1966) concentrates on an even more limited period of time, dealing in depth with 39 periodicals being published in the years 1756-1763.

For the history of the periodical in the United States there are the five volumes of Frank Luther Mott's *A history of American magazines* (Cambridge, Mass, Belknap P of Harvard UP, 1930-1968), each of which is devoted to a particular period: vol 1 covering 1741-1850, vol 2 1850-1865, vol 3 1865-1885, vol 4 1885-1905, and vol 5 1905-1930 (with a cumulative index to all five volumes). The eminence of this work is epitomised in Howard Mumford Jones's foreword to the last volume as follows: 'You cannot think of the history of the Roman empire without thinking of Gibbon, and you cannot think of the history of the magazine in our country without thinking of Mott, the first book you turn to, the latest you consult'.

To return to English periodicals: Francis Jeffrey began his article in the *Edinburgh review* on Wordsworth's *Excursion* (1814) with, 'This will never do'. The same sort of severity can still be found today. In the *Times literary supplement* for September 1 1966, a review began, 'Owners of high-powered magnifying glasses will find much to reward them in Douglas Bush's edition of Milton's poetry'. The *TLS*, with its magisterial tone, seems to span that century and a half since the *Edinburgh review*. It forms another kind of bridge also, between general, non-academic periodicals like *Books and bookmen,* and scholarly journals such as the *Review of English studies*. Being weekly, it appears sufficiently frequently to provide a 'current awareness' service to the librarian; and since it also carries advertisements for library posts, it is regarded by the profession almost as its trade paper.

The *TLS*, according to its fiftieth anniversary number, 'started as a makeshift and continued through an oversight'; as *The times* began to contain more and more book reviews, the *Supplement* appeared 'in order to keep abreast with the more important publications of the day'. Its first editor was J R Thursfield, and then, for nearly forty years, it was edited by Sir Bruce Richmond. Aiming at 'a detached appraisal', it hoped to speak with 'a voice which we hope is that of the civilized man, decided but not nagging, accurate but not prim, open to argument, readier to persuade than to convict'.

One of the *TLS*'s major principles is maintaining the anonymity of its reviewers, despite criticism such as that by F W Bateson (in *Essays in criticism* for 1957) who insists that 'the reviewer's name is an essential part of the meaning of the review'. The other quarrel Bateson has with the *TLS* is in regard to its tendency to be anti-American. Otherwise, Bateson is prepared to regard it as an 'indispensable . . . feature of our culture', praising it for its scholarliness, and for the good quality of its writing, which he characterizes as 'a diffused perfection'.

The core of the *TLS* is its book reviews, but in addition it offers a front-page article based on an important work or works, a fiction page or pages, an editorial, letters (usually lively), poems, a *Books received* section (classified under subject headings), notes on sales, and articles on bibliographical matters, current periodicals, manuscripts, book-collecting, book design and production, publishing, exhibitions and collections.

Books and bookmen has already been mentioned. This is a monthly current guide for the general reader on fiction and popular non-fiction. It contains up to a hundred short reviews, lists best-sellers, and features illustrated interviews with authors. *British book news*, published monthly by the British Council, is also geared mainly to book reviews, offering about 250 of them in a comprehensive Commonwealth coverage. *The bookseller* is the weekly trade journal, with publishing and bookselling news, and lists of all new publications. *The bookman* reviews the monthly choice of the Book Society, which issues it.

The above may be regarded as the librarian's bread-and-butter publications, their main function being listing and reviewing current books. Forming a completely different category are the contemporary critical and cultural journals. *Encounter*, monthly, is one of these, dealing with literature, the arts and current affairs, and publishing original poems and stories; it also contains book reviews. Another is the *Critical quarterly*, with long critical articles, critical analyses of single poems, original poetry, and long reviews of literary works. From America, in this category, come the *Partisan review*, the *Hudson review*, and the *Sewanee review*. The *London magazine*, monthly, devoted to the arts in general, belongs to the same group; while the *Contemporary review*, the *Quarterly review* and *Twentieth century* (formerly *Nineteenth century*), continue their traditional surveys of contemporary arts and affairs.

In less expansive format, more topically, and on a weekly basis, the same sort of function is performed by the *Listener*, the *New statesman*, the *Spectator* and *Time and tide*; not to mention such Sunday newspapers as the *Observer* and the *Sunday times*. All, in their turn, contain book reviews.

It is worth considering at this point just what periodicals offer to the librarian of a collection of literature in English. From only those mentioned so far, he has already obtained lists and reviews of new publications; a knowledge of what is happening in the book trade generally, in bookselling and in publishing; an awareness of what is happening culturally; examples of contemporary creative writing; experience of current critical assessments; and in general terms of the service he offers personally as a librarian, an acquaintance with current events and preoccupations on all fronts.

The librarian of a large collection of literature in English relies heavily on another category of periodicals: the scholarly journals. It goes without saying that in a university library, for example, a comprehensive holding of these is vital. The *Review of English studies* (1925-), has already been mentioned. This is a quarterly, published by Oxford UP, containing critical articles and reviews. Other important examples are: *ELH: a journal of English literary history* (1934-); *English studies: a journal of English letters and philology* (Amsterdam, 1919-); *Essays in criticism* (1951-); and the *Modern language review: a journal devoted to the study of medieval and modern literature and philology* (1905-). America has supplied some mighty titles also: *Modern language quarterly* (Seattle, Washington UP, 1940-); *Modern philology* (Chicago, Chicago UP, 1903-); *Philological quarterly* (University of Iowa, 1922-); *PMLA* (*Publications of the Modern Language Association of America*, 1884/5-); and *Studies in philology* (North Carolina UP, 1906-). Three annual volumes of critical articles are the English Association's *Essays and studies* (Oxford, Clarendon P, 1910-); *English institute essays* (New York, Columbia UP, 1940-); and the Royal Society of Literature's *Essays by divers hands* (1825-).

A further category of periodicals are those devoted to bibliography. The oldest of these is *The library: transactions of the Bibliographical Society* (1889-), a quarterly concerned with bibliographical research. A relatively recent example is *The bibliotheck, a Scottish journal of bibliography and allied topics,* published by the Scottish Group of the University and Research Section of the Library Association, since 1956. From America, there are the *Papers of the Bibliographical Society of America* (1904/5), and *Studies in bibliography: papers of the Bibliographical Society of the University of Virginia* (1948/9-). There are also the *Transactions* of the Cambridge Bibliographical Society (1949-).

The groups of periodicals discussed so far are, by and large, general in their coverage. A final category are those which specialize: either nationally, or by period, or by form, or even by being concerned only with one particular writer.

An example of national specialization is *American literature*

(1929-), a quarterly published by Duke UP and the American Literature Group of the Modern Language Association of America, containing historical, critical and bibliographical articles, book reviews, lists of dissertations in progress, and a bibliography of articles on American literature appearing in current periodicals; Lewis Leary's very useful *Articles on American literature, 1900-1950* (Durham, NC, Duke UP, 1954) is based principally on the bibliographies published in *American literature* but with the addition of older periodical references back to 1900. Another example of national specialization is *Canadian literature* (1959-), published by the University of British Columbia at Vancouver and containing critical articles, book reviews, and a yearly bibliography of Canadian literature. A further example is the *Journal of Commonwealth literature* (1965-), which also provides an annual bibliography of its field.

Turning to periodicals concerned with particular periods, two specialist journals for the Middle English period are: *Speculum: a journal of medieval studies* (Cambridge, Mass, 1926-), which apart from articles on the culture of the medieval period, and book reviews, also has in each issue a bibliography of articles appearing in American periodicals; and *Medium aevum* (1932-), published semi-annually by Basil Blackwell for the Society for the Study of Mediaeval Languages and Literature. A further example of this kind of specialization is *Victorian studies* (Bloomington, Indiana University, 1957-), which as well as articles and book reviews for the Victorian period also provides annually a bibliography of Victorian studies.

Three examples of periodicals specializing in a literary form are: *Modern drama* (Lawrence, Kan, University of Kansas, 1958-), covering all countries and again providing an annual bibliography in its field; *Modern fiction studies* (Lafayette, Ind, Purdue University, 1955-), a scholarly quarterly concerned with English, American and European fiction since 1880, also providing bibliographies of current work; and, a combination of form and period specialization, *Nineteenth-century fiction* (Berkeley, California UP, 1945-). For poetry, there are a host of little magazines whose main purpose is to print original work; the *Critical quarterly,* already noted, is particularly strong on poetry; and *The Explicator* (1942-) with its short articles analysing and explaining poetry and fiction is more concerned with the first.

Shakespeare is an obvious candidate for a journal of specialist studies; since 1950 there has been the *Shakespeare quarterly,* published by the Shakespeare Association, New York, with critical articles and reviews, and an annual bibliography; and on this side of the Atlantic, there is the annual *Shakespeare survey* (1948-), published by Cambridge UP for the University of Birmingham, the University of Manchester, the Shakespeare Memorial Theatre, and the Shakespeare Birthday Trust. Also well-known is the *Keats-Shelley journal* (New York, Keats-Shelley Association of America, 1952-), concerned with these two poets, Byron, Leigh Hunt, and their circle, and again providing an annual bibliography of pertinent studies. Other examples are: *The Dickensian* (1905-), published by the Dickens Fellowship; the *Kipling journal* (1927-), quarterly from the Kipling Society; *The Shavian* (1953-), semi-annually from the Shaw Society; and *The Wellsian* (1960-), six times a year from the H G Wells Society. In the same category, are the *Transactions* of the Brontë Society, and those of the Johnson Society, and the *Report* of the Jane Austen Society.

The intention of these few pages on periodicals has been to survey the field and to give some examples of the various categories, but a librarian, in addition to an overall picture of what is available, needs also exhaustive periodical guides and indexes if he is to exploit, and if his users are to exploit, this important material.

A first need is to be able to trace and identify periodicals, and to locate actual runs. In Britain, the standard list is the *British union-catalogue of periodicals of the world, from the seventeenth century to the present day, in British libraries* (London, Butterworth, 4 vols, 1955-8; supplement, 1962), known best by its initials, *BUCOP.* As can be seen from its sub-title, it is an actual location list, the most comprehensive ever published, itemizing over 140,000 titles held in 441 libraries. A new-style *BUCOP* is now in progress, with entry invariably under title, rather than as previously, sometimes under issuing body; and a quarterly and annual continuation, *New periodical titles,* produced by computer print-out. *BUCOP* is the foundation of the periodicals inter-library loan system in this country. The standard routine for a librarian when he is asked to obtain an

English studies periodical not in the stock of his own library is to look up that periodical in *BUCOP* and so ascertain which library to apply to for the loan of it, or for a photocopy of the required article in it. In the United States and Canada, the equivalent of *BUCOP* is the *Union list of serials in libraries of the United States and Canada* (New York, Wilson, 3rd ed, 5 vols, 1965), which records over 120,000 titles located in about 650 libraries, in a detailed, scholarly fashion.

While both *BUCOP* and the *Union list* are concerned with actual runs of periodicals, whether current or extinct, *Ulrich's International periodicals directory* (New York, Bowker, 13th ed, 2 vols, 1969) lists only periodicals which are being published and are obtainable currently. It is a list of approximately 40,000 titles, giving for each its date of inception, its frequency, its price, and the address from which it can be obtained. The periodicals are classified by subject, and there is a title index. The coverage is international. In David Woodworth's *Guide to current British journals* (London, Library Association 1970) some 2,850 periodicals are classified according to the Universal Decimal Classification, and described; the information provided in each of the entries includes date of first issue, previous titles and dates, frequency, level of appeal (using symbols —for example □ represents 'research'), coverage, and special features. An appendix lists journals carrying abstracts, and there is an index of titles. Also of use in identifying periodicals are three annual commercial directories: *The newspaper press directory* (London, Benn, 1846-), also known as *Mitchell's* after its former publisher, the periodical entries in which give the standard information as to frequency, price, publisher, and so on; *Willing's press guide* (London, Willing, 1871-), covering the United Kingdom, and principal Commonwealth and foreign publications; and *The writers' and artists' year book* (London, Black, 1906-), which is very familiar to aspiring writers, since, among other things, it describes briefly the subject coverage (and therefore the market potentiality) of British and American periodicals, along with the usual publication details.

The above lists identify and/or locate periodicals, and give some guidance as to their general character and coverage, but for an analysis of the articles contained in this multitude, recourse must

92

be made to periodical abstracts and indexes. In a sense, much of the ground has already been covered in this textbook, since the majority of the standard works which have been reviewed contain numerous references to important material in periodicals. Also, as has been noted in the present chapter, periodicals—especially those specializing in a particular period, form or author—very often themselves offer regular lists and indexes of periodical articles. The *PMLA* annual bibliography is an outstanding general example.

There is in the field one abstracting journal: *Abstracts of English studies* (Boulder, University of Colorado, 1958-), which appears monthly and abstracts more than 200 current journals.

The best-known periodical index produced in the United Kingdom is the Library Association's *British humanities index*, known as such since 1962, and previously (1915-) as the *Subject index to periodicals*. The *Social sciences and humanities index* (New York, H W Wilson, 1916; formerly the *International index*), covers from 1907 to the present and indexes about 175 American and English scholarly journals. Also from the H W Wilson Company is the *Readers' guide to periodical literature* (1905-), indexing popular American titles. W F Poole's *An index to periodical literature, 1802-1881* (Boston, Houghton, 4th ed, 2 vols, 1891; with supplements covering 1882-1906), indexes 479 English and American periodicals by subject or title. Finally, mention may be made of the monthly *Canadian periodical index* (Ottawa, Canadian Library Association, 1964-; previously, *Canadian index to periodicals and documentary films*), which cumulates annually, and comprises an author and subject index to sixty or so Canadian periodicals in all fields.

The Wellesley index to Victorian periodicals, 1824-1900, edited by Walter E Houghton, has recently begun to appear (vol 1, London, Routledge, 1966). This extremely valuable and important work indexes eight leading Victorian periodicals, in three sections: first, contributions arranged chronologically under each periodical; second, an alphabetical index of the writers, listing their contributions; and third, an index of pseudonyms and initials. A second volume of this work will cover about thirty other periodicals similarly. Also relating to the Victorian period is Andrew Boyle's *An index to the annuals;* only vol 1 has been published so far (Worcester, Andrew Boyle Booksellers Ltd, 1967), and this lists in alphabetical order the authors who between 1820 and 1850 contributed to those yearly decorative volumes which embody all that characterizes early Victoriana. Under each author is given a list of contributions, arranged by name of annual.

CHAPTER X

Micro-reproductions, manuscripts and theses

'EVEN THE SMALLEST LIBRARY can have a complete collection of early English and American literature. For peanuts.'

So read an advertisement on behalf of University Microfilms Inc, in *College and research libraries*. 'For peanuts' is a very relative term, because micro-reproductions are not inexpensive; but it is true in the sense that what can now be obtained for a collection of literature in English in the form of microfilm, micro-card or micro-fiche would otherwise be totally unobtainable and therefore beyond price. The advertisement went on to offer, on microfilm, every title in Pollard and Redgrave (all books published in England from 1475 to 1640); every title in Wing (all books published in England from 1641 to 1700); a complete collection of British essays, journals and magazines of the seventeenth, eighteenth and nineteenth centuries; and every American novel published between 1774 and 1865.

The same firm, which is based at Ann Arbor, Michigan, but which also operates in London as University Microfilms Limited, in addition runs an out-of-print book programme, so that by a combination of microfilming and xerographic printing, a copy of any out-of-print item can be supplied by them, either from their catalogue or by special request. The method is that the original is microfilmed and a xerographic print made on a continuous roll of paper. The pages are then cut, and bound in hard or paper covers. In practical terms, this means that if the money is available, any library can obtain any book. The growing importance of micro-reproduction is illustrated by this statement from the *Foreword* to one of their catalogues: 'We are privileged to maintain a micro-film camera in the British Museum Photographic Studio where we can microfilm books, music, manuscripts, letters etc, which, subject to copyright, can be reproduced by xerography'. University Micro-films have likewise penetrated Keats House at Hampstead, to film the Keats papers; and the William Wordsworth and G K Chesterton papers are also obtainable from them.

The logical step from this is that the librarian of a large and important collection of literature in English should equip his own library with a microfilm or microfiche camera, so that he can make copies of works from other libraries available in his own library and in turn make copies of items in his stock available to others. It also goes without saying that he must have an ordinary book-copying machine for standard-size reproductions. The greatest value of such a machine lies in its making possible the reproduction, for study purposes, of articles from scholarly periodicals—always, of course, bearing in mind the restrictions of the copyright law.

The University Microfilms advertisement emphasized only one aspect of micro-reproduction: the making available of rare, or unique, or otherwise unobtainable items for a collection. The other aspect of micro-reproduction, plainly deducible from its name, is that it is above all a method of miniaturization. When the Readex Microprint Corporation's project of recording in microprint three centuries of English and American drama was first suggested, it was this aspect which appealed to George Freedley, the President of the Theatre Library Association, who wrote: ' The idea of having five thousand plays available in a case no larger than a man's shoe box caught my imagination '. This project has now been carried out, and the set of over five thousand plays is currently available, divided into the following chronological groups:

1516-1641   Elizabethan, Shakespeare, Jacobean
1642-1700   Restoration drama
1701-1750   Early eighteenth century
1751-1800   Late eighteenth century
1737-1800   Larpent MS. plays
1741-1830   American plays.

This collection has been supplemented by a further series, of nineteenth century English and American plays. The checklist, produced by G W Bergquist, to accompany the ' three centuries ' collection, has already been described, in chapter IV. Another major undertaking by Readex has been the filming of ' the complete text of every existent book, pamphlet, and broadside printed in the United States in the years 1639 through 1800 '.

The advantages of miniaturization are manifold, but there are inconveniences also. When microfilm was first introduced, the immediate attack was on long runs of bulky newspapers: *The times* in particular. In the basement of practically every library in the land a great deal of space and a great deal of special shelving was taken up with a long set of this newspaper. The volumes were expensive to bind, and when bound, back-breaking to handle. To substitute a few shelves of boxed microfilms for all this bulk, expense and back-ache was an undoubted blessing. It will be noted, however, that all these were administrative advantages: fine for the library and the library staff, but what of the user? The truth is that for the researcher scanning newspapers in pursuit of material, the conventional bound volumes were a great deal more satisfactory to consult. The main reason was that the human eye, assisted by the human hand, could survey the extensive area of a newspaper page more selectively and therefore more rapidly than was possible on the microfilm readers then available; also, scrutiny for a long spell of the actual printed page was less arduous on the eyes than focusing closely for the same length of time on the illuminated glass screen of a microfilm reader. In those enthusiastic days, the library of the future was visualized as a medium-sized microfilm store. This has never happened: the current, and more likely library of the future is a large computer.

In essence, the argument of this last paragraph is that micro-reproductions are to be approached with some care. They are administratively very attractive: items can be obtained in micro-form which would otherwise be out of reach, and because of the compact form, stored in considerable numbers. But the librarian has also to think of his users. When he can afford to buy and house the original, or a standard-size copy or facsimile of the original, then he should do so. Where he supplies a micro-reproduction, he must protect his users. The first need here is the provision of a wide range of very good readers, both the large, standard models (such as the Recordak Archival Reader), and the truly portable kind for private use. He must store his microfilms efficiently: if, as was narrated previously, at one period every library housed in its basement the endless bulky volumes of *The times*, the next period, it may be added, saw every library in the land in gingerly custody of a mystery-shrouded cupboard of microfilm reels. Such a microfilm store should be properly and methodically arranged, and its items recorded in the library's catalogue. Another service which the librarian should offer his users is the making, if required, of standard-size reproductions of a part or of the whole of a microfilm; reader-printers for this purpose, expensive but foolproof, are already on the market.

Micro Methods Limited, of East Ardsley, Wakefield, Yorkshire, is a British firm active in the field of micro-reproduction. Its prospectus reminds the librarian of the various kinds of microform. Microfilm is the most familiar. Reels of 35mm or 16mm film are used; a full 100-feet reel of 35mm film could record 600 pages of newspaper; on 16mm film, 2,400 crown octavo ($7\frac{1}{4}$ in by $4\frac{7}{8}$ in) pages can be contained in the same length. A microfiche is a flat transparent sheet of film, 3in by 5in, on which thirty or forty pages can be reproduced. A micro-card is similar to a microfiche, but opaque. There are also variations of the three forms, such as jacketed strip microfilm; but microfilm is still the most common form, with microfiche tipped as being likely to displace it as far as books are concerned.

Microfilm is most suitable for recording long runs of newspapers and journals, and is essential for books which may need to be enlarged by the xerox process at some future date. Microfiche and micro-card are most suitable for out-of-print books, unpublished theses, and items needed for reference purposes.

The catalogue of Micro Methods Limited is another which will be of interest to the librarian of a collection of literature in English. It offers microfilms of manuscripts—for example, of the Caedmon Manuscript; colour microfilms of William Blake's illuminated books; a microfilm of the collection of original letters of Charles Dickens in the Dickens House; reproductions of theses—for example, those from the Department of English, Leeds University; and periodicals, such as *Encounter,* 1953-60, in thirteen reels.

Microcard Editions Inc, of Washington DC, will supply micro-cards or microfilms of periodicals, such as *Anglia*; of collections, such as Dodsley's *Select collection of old plays,* or the Early English Text Society's publications; and of facsimiles, such as the *Shakespeare quarto facsimiles.*

Manuscripts have been mentioned in the course of reviewing what is obtainable in the form of microfilm, because most collections of literature in English do not, of course, possess original older manuscript material. In such libraries as do possess them, manuscripts are not regarded as part of the ordinary collections, but are separately housed and administered. Thus the nearest acquaintance a general librarian is likely to have with manuscripts is by way of microfilm reproductions, or by facsimiles, or by catalogues of manuscript holdings. Even his connection by way of facsimiles will be slight, since for all but the largest libraries, facsimiles are too expensive. An important example of the publication of facsimiles of manuscripts is the series *Early English manuscripts in facsimile* (Copenhagen, Rosenkilde and Bagger, 1951-), the handsome volumes of which are likely to grace the shelves of most research collections.

Two catalogues of manuscripts have already been noted (in chapter IV): Ker's *Catalogue of manuscripts containing Anglo-Saxon,* and Heusinkveld and Bashe's *Bibliographical guide to Old English.* The greatest collection of manuscripts in Britain is at the British Museum, and the best guide to its catalogues of manuscripts is T C Skeat's *The catalogues of the manuscript collections in the British Museum* (British Museum, rev ed, 1962), which lists, with annotations, the printed and manuscript catalogues of the collection of Western manuscripts in the Department of Manuscripts. The foundation of the British Museum's collection was the Sloane MSS, purchased in 1753 from the executors of Sir Hans Sloane; and what are known as the 'Additional MSS' are all those acquired by the department after that date, their numeration following on that of the Sloane (numbered from 1 to 4,100), beginning with 4,101. The published catalogue of the collections is the *Catalogue of additions to the Department of Manuscripts since 1782* (British Museum, 11 vols, 1831-36), which was preceded by Samuel Ayscough's *A catalogue of the manuscripts preserved in the British Museum* (2 vols, 1782), and followed by *Index to the Additional Manuscripts . . . 1783-1835* (1849); subsequently, there are a whole series of volumes entitled *Catalogue of additions,* covering 1830-39 (1830-39), 1836-40 (1843), 1841-45 (1850), 1846-7 (1864), 1848-53 (1868), 1854-60 (1875), 1861-75 (1877), 1876-81 (1882), 1882-87 (1889), 1888-93

(1894), 1894-99 (1903), 1900-05 (1907), 1906-10 (1912), 1911-15 (1925), 1916-20 (1933), 1921-25 (1950), 1926-30 (1959), 1931-35 (1967), and 1936-45 (2 vols, 1970).

The other great collection of manuscripts in this country is at the Bodleian and the printed catalogue here is *A summary catalogue of western manuscripts in the Bodleian Library at Oxford,* by R W Hunt and others (Oxford, 8 vols, 1895-1953); there is also Margaret Crum's *First-line index of English poetry 1500-1800 in manuscripts of the Bodleian Library, Oxford* (Oxford, Clarendon P, 2 vols, 1969), which includes references to about 23,000 poems from manuscripts, with bibliographical and historical notes, and indexes of authors, names mentioned and composers of musical settings. Cambridge is represented by H P Luard's *A catalogue of the manuscripts preserved in the library of the University of Cambridge* (Cambridge, Cambridge UP, 5 vols, 1856-67), and A E B Owen's *Summary guide to accessions of Western manuscripts . . . since 1867* (Cambridge, Cambridge UP, 1966). From the Historical Manuscripts Commission there is *A guide to the reports on collections of manuscripts of private families, corporations and institutions in Great Britain and Ireland* (London, 3 vols, 1914-38); and for material of Scottish interest there is the National Library of Scotland's *Catalogue of manuscripts acquired since 1925* (vols 1-3, Edinburgh, 1938-1968).

On the other side of the Atlantic, there is Seymour de Ricci's *Census of medieval and renaissance manuscripts in the United States and Canada* (New York, 3 vols, 1935-40, recently reprinted by the Kraus Reprint Corporation, 1961-2; with a supplement by C U Faye and W H Bond, 1962). The manuscripts are listed library by library, and then described and numbered. The libraries are arranged alphabetically within each city, and each city is arranged alphabetically within each state. Another guide to American manuscripts is *American literary manuscripts: a checklist of holdings in academic, historical and public libraries in the United States* (Austin, Texas UP, 1960), which was compiled, under the auspices of the American Literature Group of the Modern Language Association of America, by the Committee on Manuscript Holdings. Authors' names are listed alphabetically, and under each are given one or more library symbols—for example, ICN: that is, the Newberry Library (N), in the city of Chicago (C), in the state of Illinois (I);

there are also symbols indicating categories of material—for example, J indicating journals, and L indicating letters. Two other guides to manuscripts in America are Philip M Harmer's *A guide to archives and manuscripts in the United States* (New Haven, Yale UP, 1961); and *The national union catalog of manuscript collections, 1959-1961* (Ann Arbor, Edwards, 1962). The latter has been continued by *The national union catalog of manuscript collections, 1962,* and an *Index, 1959-62* (Hamden, Conn, Shoe String P, 1964). Linking the two countries is *A guide to manuscripts relating to America in Great Britain and Ireland,* by B R Crick and Miriam Alman (London, Oxford UP, 1961).

The firm of University Microfilms, mentioned at the very beginning of this chapter, publishes regularly *Dissertation abstracts international,* a guide to dissertations available on microfilm, and has done so since 1938. The original title (1938-51) was *Microfilm abstracts.* This publication is an indication of the increasing importance of these two kinds of material—micro-reproductions and theses—and the way they have become linked. It was also noted earlier, that the British firm of Micro Methods publishes the theses of the Leeds University Department of English on microfilm.

Theses, or dissertations, have always been important. Very often, they are the forerunners or originals of what subsequently appear as books, but in most cases they remain in typescript and are preserved only in the library of the university under whose wing the research was conducted. Hence the value of two kinds of recent development: first, the publication of lists of theses in progress or completed; and second, the actual publication now of many theses, not by conventional methods—impossible economically because of the limited demand—but by micro-reproduction. The first of these developments becomes more and more justified each year, as the number of degree students grows, and the number going into postgraduate research—and producing theses therefore—grows in its turn.

Published annually by Aslib since 1953, has been the *Index of theses accepted for higher degrees in the universities of Great Britain and Ireland.* The first volume covered the academic year 1950-1; details given are author's name, university, degree, and title of thesis; the arrangement is a classified one, with author and

101

subject heading indexes. Individual universities, such as Oxford, Cambridge and London, also publish lists of their theses.

Dissertation abstracts international has already been noted. Arrangement is by subject, in two sections: A, the Humanities and Social Sciences; and B, the Sciences and Engineering. Each issue has a keyword title and author index; and for each dissertation a 600-word abstract is given. More than 250 American and Canadian institutions are covered, and the inclusion of dissertations from European universities is projected. University Microfilms now offer a nine-volume retrospective index to the entire 1938-June 1969 period, in which the keywords of the 150,000 dissertations abstracted are listed alphabetically; each of the first eight volumes of the index encompasses a broad subject area (Literature being dealt with as part of vol VIII), with vol IX providing an author index to the whole. Another yearly list is *Doctoral dissertations accepted by American universities, 1933/4-* (New York, Wilson, 1934-); before this, the Library of Congress's *A list of American doctoral dissertations printed in 1912-38* (Washington, Government Printing Office, 26 vols, 1912-40), is to be consulted.

Devoted entirely to the field of English is Lawrence F Mac-Namee's *Dissertations in English and American literature: theses accepted by American, British and German universities, 1865-1964* (New York, Bowker, 1968). This large (1,124 pages) computer-produced volume is arranged in 35 chapters, each of which is concerned with a particular period or topic (for example, chapter 11 is on the Victorian age, and chapter 32 is on negro literature); in most chapters there are a hundred subdivisions, the first fourteen of which are parallel where possible—thus 0411 is humour in the Middle English period, and 5011 is humour in the American colonial period. Each entry consists of the author and title of the thesis, the year, and the code number of the university. The volume begins with a list of university codes (for example, 110 Boston, 504 Bristol, 888 Berlin); a list of subject codes (for example, the ballad in America, 7014); and an index to major authors. At the end of the volume there is a ' cross-index of authors ' which picks up names of historical figures and of authors treated collectively or secondarily, and an 'Alphabetical listing of authors of dissertations '.

Two American lists of theses of especial interest in the field are:

James Woodress's *Dissertations in American literature, 1891-1966* (Durham, NC, Duke UP, 1968), in which, following dissertations on individual writers arranged alphabetically, entries are grouped under topics such as drama, fiction, language, the negro; and Richard D Altick and William R Matthews's *Guide to doctoral dissertations in Victorian literature, 1886-1958* (Urbana, Illinois UP, 1960).

Two lists from the Commonwealth countries are: D L Jenkins's *Union list of theses of the University of New Zealand, 1910-1954* (Wellington, New Zealand Library Association, 1956); and M J Marshall's *Union list of higher degree theses in Australian university libraries* (Hobart, University of Tasmania Library, 1959; *Supplement*, 1959-), in which over 3,000 theses are arranged into subject classes.

Restrictions on the consultation or borrowing of theses are usually quite severe: very properly so, since a thesis is the product of a prolonged period of original research and distinctly the property of its author. It would be wrong to make it possible for one researcher to benefit unfairly from work carried out by another. A further point is that most authors of theses hope eventually to publish the results of their work in one form or another. On the other hand, a librarian in whose library theses have been deposited would be remiss if he did not try to arrange legitimate, authorized consultation or loan of such theses where possible. Most of the lists of theses cited in this chapter give some indication of their availability.

CHAPTER XI

Selection

THE BASIS OF BOOK SELECTION is book information. The first phase of this information comes from current bibliographies: from the regular routine perusal of publications such as the *British national bibliography* and *The bookseller*. The second phase arises from the reading of book reviews. A third and daily phase is scanning the contents of incoming publishers' and booksellers' catalogues. A fourth, background phase is the retrospective checking and augmenting of stock suggested by the consultation of standard selective and comprehensive bibliographies. All of these are on the librarian's own initiative; but in most libraries selection is also done by the users in that they recommend to the librarian that particular items be added to stock.

The checking and marking-up of the weekly lists is the core of an acquisitions routine. With the *British national bibliography,* since it is classified by subject, this is a simple matter. A very rapid glance indeed at the bibliography, language, literature, fiction and biography classes is sufficient to inform the librarian of a collection of literature in English of the current important British publications in the field. Some items, for which there is an unanswerable case, he can mark for purchase immediately. In the case of others, he may wish to seek a second opinion, or read a review when a review appears, or hold back temporarily for financial reasons. No matter what his system of priorities, he is still likely to base his work on such a list or lists; and eventually, at a much later stage, to check back through all his markings to complete the whole operation. The other reason why such lists are the main tools in an acquisitions routine is that prior to ordering any item from a bookseller the librarian must establish precise publication details, and these lists supply them, along with works such as Whitaker's *British books in print* and Bowker's *Books in print,* mentioned in chapter IV.

104

A librarian's use of book reviews is an equivocal business. On the one hand, he relies on them to provide a gloss on what until then is only a title; on the other, he is in no way committed to accept the opinions contained in them, and may very well choose to ignore their strictures, or even their praises. The periodicals cited in chapter IX, without exception, offer book reviews in the field of literature in English. The main group includes the *Times literary supplement, Books and bookmen* and *British book news.* Book reviews also appear in the more general, cultural periodicals: *Encounter,* the *Partisan review* and the *Critical quarterly* are examples here. A third group providing book reviews are the scholarly journals: the *Review of English studies, ELH,* and the *Philological quarterly,* among others. A point worth adding is that the above groupings in effect provide a time sequence: reviews appear earliest in publications such as *Books and bookmen;* then in the more general periodicals; and finally, often a very long time after, in the scholarly journals.

In many instances, initially, all the librarian has in the way of information about a particular book is its author and title, and this is not usually a sufficient basis on which to make a decision about purchasing it. Hence his reliance on reviews, which will indicate its coverage, its level, and its worth. He is more concerned with these first two elements than the last: in the end, only he can decide whether a book merits a place in his library. Book reviews can be superficial, distorted, prejudiced, or excuses for exhibitionist erudition. They need not always be apt: for example, the librarian of a public library lending department does not choose his fiction according to the critical criteria of an F R Leavis. Sometimes a librarian has to ignore a bad review: if the latest novel of an eminent, popular and well-established author is dismissed as worthless, the librarian is usually still obliged to buy it. Similarly, what a reviewer considers a bad book on a subject might still be the only book on that subject and therefore has to be purchased.

The *Book review digest* (New York, Wilson, 1905-) is a monthly guide, with annual and five-yearly cumulations, to the reviews appearing in English and American periodicals. It is arranged alphabetically by the author of the book reviewed, and gives references to and extracts from reviews; it includes a subject, title, and pseudo-

105

nym index. A similar, and to some extent overlapping, publication is *An index to book reviews in the humanities* (Detroit, Phillip Thomson, 1960-), which appears quarterly and which covers reviews in about 500 periodicals; entries again are arranged by the author of the book reviewed, and the author, title, publisher, date and page of the review are given.

The librarian of any collection of literature in English must become familiar with the various publishing houses in his field. The worth of a particular book can normally be guaged by the reputation of its publisher. Knowing something of the background of publishing helps. The standard historical treatment is Frank Arthur Mumby's *Publishing and bookselling: a history from the earliest times to the present day* (London, Cape, 4th ed, 1956), which in addition contains the fullest bibliography of the subject. This bibliography makes an especial feature of listing publishing firms—Batsford, Bentley, Blackie, Blackwood, Cassell, Collins, Dent, Longman, Macmillan and the rest—alphabetically by name and giving references to histories of them. The *Times literary supplement* also takes an interest in histories of publishing houses.

A librarian's very first step in this area is to arrange that he receives publishers' catalogues. This is a simple matter. If he turns to his copy of the *Writers' and artists' year book* he will find most of the important British and American publishers listed, with a statement of the subject fields in which they specialize. All he needs then to do is to mark the appropriate firms and have a postcard sent to each requesting the regular mailing of catalogues. The usual result is a steady seasonal flow of publishing information.

Constant acquaintance with books in the field of literature in English gradually builds up in the librarian's mind a character study of each publisher. From Faber, for example, he expects a strong line in poetry, especially modern poetry (Eliot, Auden, Pound, de la Mare, Larkin, Ted Hughes) and literary criticism (Sir Herbert Read is an instance). From Gollancz, a great deal of fiction—humorous, detective—mostly American in origin; as well as the works of Colin Wilson, I Compton-Burnett, and D L Sayers. From Heinemann, good collected fiction including many of the modern great names—Maugham, Priestley, D H Lawrence, Graham Greene; drama—Noel Coward; and poetry—Masefield, Richard

106

Church. From Calder, avante-garde contemporary literature—Beckett, for example.

A very special place in his regard will go to the Oxford University Press. A glance even at the index of this present textbook under *Oxford* will indicate just how important this press is in the field of literature in English. Unanswerable proof of its importance is best obtained by an examination of its massive annual catalogue, which unlike most publishers' catalogues, has to be purchased. Oxford, first of all, publishes a host of reference works and anthologies: the *Oxford* dictionaries, the *Oxford* companions, the *Oxford* books of verse. Secondly, it publishes important periodicals: the *Review of English studies, Notes and queries,* and *English.* Thirdly, it publishes society publications: those of the Early English Text Society, the Chaucer Society, and the Society for Pure English. Fourthly, it publishes literary history and criticism: the outstanding example being the *Oxford history of English literature.* And fifthly, and most importantly, it publishes a vast range of texts. There are the *Oxford English texts,* ' library editions handsomely printed on good paper, the text constituted by critical recension of the original printings collated with such MSS as are extant '; the *Oxford standard authors,* inexpensive but accurate texts; the *Oxford English novels;* and the multitudinous *World's classics* ' offering in small compass and at low price the most famous works in the English language '.

It is difficult not to regard the catalogues of second-hand booksellers as snares and delusions, but even so a librarian must have them. To obtain addresses and details he can consult *A directory of dealers in secondhand and antiquarian books in the British Isles, 1964-66* (London, Sheppard Press, 1965), which contains a general information section, a geographical section, an alphabetical index, a speciality index, and a permanent wants index. For the British Isles there is also *The complete booksellers directory (mainly antiquarian)* (Wilbarston, Market Harborough, Gerald Coe, 1969), again with geographical, alphabetical and speciality indexes; whilst an international coverage is provided by the *World directory of booksellers* (London, A P Wales, 1970), though this gives little more than addresses.

Sometimes it seems that there are only two kinds of dealers' catalogues, and both are wasteful: the opulent, and the messy. The opulent is glossy, illustrated and magnificently printed; what spoils its charms for the librarian is the realization that, as with all advertisement, in the end it is he who is paying for it in the inflated prices of the items offered. The messy kind are stencilled, crammed, and notoriously inaccurate in their details. The waste here is of the librarian's time and eyesight. The prices need not be inflated to make the consultation of such catalogues uneconomical: all the librarian need do is to calculate, in terms of salary, how much work is involved in sieving and checking in pursuit of two or three items, which in any case—if the catalogue has been delayed—will probably have already been sold.

All librarians have to maintain a desiderata file of items which are out of print but very much wanted by their libraries. Hence the need for booksellers' catalogues. The items in such a desiderata file should also, of course, be listed by the librarian frequently, and circulated among booksellers. Very occasionally the librarian is interested in the purchase of an expensive, and usually antiquarian, item. Guides to prices paid at auctions for such items are of value here. In this country, the two guides are: *Book prices current: a record of the prices at which books have been sold at auction from December 1886* (London, Stock, 1888-), which has three cumulative indexes for 1887-1896, 1897-1906, 1907-1916; and *Book-auction records: a priced and annotated annual record of London, New York and Edinburgh book auctions June 1902-* (London, Karslake, 1903-), which has six cumulative indexes, covering 1902-1958. In America, there is *American book-prices current: a record of library properties sold at auction in the United States* (New York, American Book-prices Current, 1895-), appearing annually, and with seven cumulative indexes covering the years 1916-1960. The Gale Research Company compiles an annual *Bookman's price index,* consolidated from the catalogues of leading English and American dealers.

Second-hand booksellers are very often able to hold librarians to ransom in the matter of out-of-print items. It is nowadays a seller's market: so many new libraries, especially new university libraries, are competing for the same items, not to mention the affluent buyers for American libraries. One result of this heavy demand for items in limited supply has been the mushroom growth of reprint firms, whose prices are better than those of the second-hand dealers, but not much better. Firms such as Johnson, Kraus, Russell and Russell, Dawson, Dover, and Burt Franklin have re-printed and are reprinting great numbers of out-of-print items, methodically and with a keen eye for the potential market. On the balance side, the rise of the paperback has filled many needs inexpensively, and practically every publisher now—including the great Oxford University Press—runs one or more paperback series.

A librarian tends to experience these difficulties with second-hand and reprint items mostly when he comes to do retrospective checking of his stock. In most libraries, the nucleus of the collection of literature in English will have been assembled several years previously. Until the librarian has examined this nucleus, category by category, period by period, form by form, author by author, he is not likely to be fully aware of its deficiencies. If he is at all dutiful, he should not wait until various users complain before discovering these deficiencies. The only real way to conduct this kind of checking is to work through appropriate selective and comprehensive biblio-graphies (described in the earlier chapters of this book).

When he has established the gaps in his stock which he would like to fill, it is then that he is likely to find that many of the works are now out of print. As mentioned earlier, he should compile a desiderata file, and search second-hand booksellers' catalogues or send out lists; but first he should check the catalogues of the reprint firms (or better still, check those lists issued by some large book-sellers of available reprints from all sources), because so much has now been reprinted.

He will also discover probably that a number of important authors are not represented in the collection, and the matter of choosing an edition of that author arises. There are two separate issues here: first and foremost, the basic worth of a particular edition; and secondly, the actual needs of his own library. There are at least five important criteria for deciding the intrinsic merits of an edition. There is the reputation of the publisher: an obvious example would be that if the publisher is the Oxford University Press, the librarian can feel confident that the edition will be a worthy one. There is the eminence of the editor: if it is by a scholar whose name is well-known to the librarian, again he can feel confident of its value. Linked with this, is the authority of the text; if the editor's competence has been established, there is little to worry about in this respect. A further factor is the appropriateness and extent of the critical apparatus. And a final, but vital point, is whether the edition really is a complete edition.

The other issue is the suitability of a particular edition as far as his users are concerned. There is no need to buy an author in the *Oxford English texts* when the *Oxford standard authors* volume would do as far as contents are concerned. In some libraries also, it would be a disservice to supply a multi-volume edition, when a one-volume version—perhaps because of an emphasis on supplying books for home reading—would be very much more convenient. There is, too, the matter of format; between two worthwhile editions the librarian of a particular library might wish to choose the more visually attractive to encourange his readers to consult it. Finally, there is the practical question of price; a librarian, with so many books to buy, cannot afford to pay more than he needs to pay.

A difficult area in which to buy, either currently or retrospectively, is that of contemporary literature. Public librarians by the very nature of the service they offer in providing everyday reading can usually afford to be more liberal in their purchase of works by contemporary writers, whereas university and college librarians are on the whole obliged to be very selective.

If the librarian of a collection of literature in English has to be selective in this area, he can apply a number of simple principles. With poetry, it is a safe policy to buy all collected editions of modern poets, since appearance in a collected edition usually indicates that a contemporary poet's worth has been established. In addition, the librarian can buy single volumes of the works of undeniably outstanding poets—Eliot, Auden, Robert Graves. Plays are best bought, not singly—which is too expensive—but in the form of contemporary anthologies or series, such as *Methuen's modern plays*. As far as novels are concerned, reviews and the consensus of modern critical opinion normally indicate which novelists are considered important. Bearing in mind that there are not more than two or three dozen such writers (English, American and

Commonwealth), the librarian should aim to buy each of their novels as they appear.

This chapter has so far been taken up with selection done on the librarian's own initiative, but he has also to deal with recommendations by his users. There is nothing but good in this if the system of recommendation does not oblige him to comply. In many university libraries there is nothing optional about a recommendation; it is a firm request which must be met. In some libraries, even, the entire book selection is done on this basis of ' recommendation ' by the academic staff, and there cannot be a worse system for a library. The obvious reason is that over the years a serious imbalance results. If the head of the English department is only interested in a particular period or in a particular form—and in these days of specialists it is usually so—he is quite likely to recommend only in that area, and to ignore the remaining periods and forms; and the incumbency of one professor can extend over two or three decades. Part of a librarian's job must be to create and maintain a balanced stock. He can only do this if he has the final say in book selection. This does not mean that he will discourage the building up by interested academics of strong specializations in the library's stock. Such specializations, since the library's function is to serve the university's individual academics as well as the university as a whole, are quite legitimate. What the librarian must do, however, is to see that such specializations are not indulged at the expense of the general coverage.

One way to avoid a dictatorial attitude by either the librarian or his users is to establish a system and atmosphere of liaison. This can be done by the transmission of book information, the basic theme of this chapter. All the forms reviewed so far—lists of new publications, book reviews, publishers' and booksellers' catalogues —can be circulated inside and outside the library, and augmented by personal contact between the librarian and his users. The atmosphere then becomes one of a co-operating team, the over-riding aim of which is to create a good collection. The librarian can bow to a user's special knowledge; the user can come to appreciate and acknowledge the librarian's problems of control, balance and finance.

A final word is in order on the question of catering for the peculiar needs of the various types of library which maintain a collection of literature in English. Firstly, too much should not be made of this. The usual contrast made is between a public library and a university library, but this is more apparent than real. The collection of literature in English in a university library, and the collection of literature in English in the reference department of a large city library ought to be almost identical. They each serve an important study and research need. The contrast between the collection in a university library and the collection in a lending or small public library is not worth labouring. One is geared entirely to research, and the other geared largely—though not of course entirely —to a general or recreational need. Their respective stocks must therefore reflect appropriately. Again, though, it is wise not to overstate the difference. A small public library should offer the English classics in an attractive format; but that is not to say that a university library should go out of its way to offer the drab and the forbidding. Equally, the very best of texts are to be expected in a university library; but it would be wickedness to offer in even the smallest library any text that was at all suspect. A collection of literature in English, in any library anywhere, ought to be assembled and maintained according to the highest standard possible. The only real variables are the size of the collection and the money available.

CHAPTER XII

Cataloguing

BECAUSE THE MATERIAL and the language are familiar, few difficulties are experienced in the cataloguing of a collection of literature in English. As far as rules for entry are concerned, only a handful are especially pertinent to the field. These are the rules, in order of importance, for pseudonyms, anonymous works, commentaries, concordances, and manuscripts. General cataloguing precepts are the same as for any other field. Ralph Waldo Emerson may have been right in every other respect when he wrote that 'A foolish consistency is the hobgoblin of little minds ', but he is to be entirely disregarded when it comes to cataloguing practice. Anything other than the strictest consistency in cataloguing is the height of foolishness; it is no hobgoblin. Cataloguing is the most demanding and the most skilled of all techniques of librarianship, and a cataloguer's unswerving respect for accuracy and consistency in the treatment of even the minutest detail is his badge of office.

The other general precept is to remember the users of the catalogue. Cataloguing rules and principles have no intrinsic value. They are but the means to an end: the successful recording, for the benefit of the library's users, of the library's books. Hence a title-page fixation on the part of the cataloguer, as opposed to a creative intention to signal all that is operative with regard to a particular volume, is to be avoided. Added entries and references should be liberally supplied. As the *ALA cataloguing rules for author and title entries* (Chicago, American Library Association, 2nd ed, 1949) noted:

' The chief function of an added entry is to enable the user of the catalogue to find a work when incomplete knowledge or imperfect memory of the work, or unfamiliarity with the rules of entry, would prevent ready access to the main entry. Added entries serve also the purpose of assembling closely related matter which has main entry under various headings.

' If it is desirable to make an added entry for a name not included in the title of the work, an explanatory note or a contents note should make the reason apparent.

' The necessity for added entries varies somewhat with the individual library and the extent to which they are made is a matter for each library to determine according to its particular needs. In general, the more indeterminate or divided the responsibility for authorship, the more need for added entries.'

The cataloguing rules now being generally adopted in Britain are the *Anglo-American cataloguing rules* (British text, London, Library Association, 1967), prepared by the American Library Association, the Library of Congress, the Library Association and the Canadian Library Association. Previously in use were the *Cataloguing rules: author and title entries* (London, Library Association, 1908), compiled by Committees of the Library Association and of the American Library Association; and the *ALA cataloging rules for author and title entries* which have already been mentioned in connection with added entries. The latter, being fuller and more scholarly, were more favoured in academic libraries. The most famous cataloguing rules of all, and historically important, are the *Rules for compiling the catalogues of printed books, maps and music in the British museum* (rev ed, 1936).

For pseudonyms, the 1967 Anglo-American code's basic rule (rule 40) applies: ' Enter a person under the name by which he is commonly identified, whether it is his real name, or an assumed name, nickname, title of nobility, or other appellation '. Rule 42 states the general principle regarding pseudonyms more specifically:

' A. If all the works of an author appear only under a single pseudonym, enter him under the pseudonym.

' B. If the works of an author appear under several pseudonyms or under his real name and one or more pseudonyms, enter him under the name by which he is primarily identified in modern editions of his works and in reference sources. In case of doubt, prefer the real name.'

It should be noted that the term ' reference sources ' is to be understood as including books and articles written about the person, rather than in the narrow sense of formal reference works. An alternative rule to replace 42B is provided to meet the needs of 'libraries in which research considerations are not paramount'. This alternative rule provides for the entry of each work under the name the author used for it, the different names under which works are entered being connected by *see also* references—the practice at present followed by the *British national bibliography*. The case of pseudonyms used jointly by two or more authors writing in collaboration is covered by rule 3C, of which the main directive is: 'If collaborating authors consistently use a joint pseudonym instead of their individual names, enter under the pseudonym and refer to it from their real names'. It is perhaps worth noting that the use of the abbreviation *pseud.* (or any other indication that the pseudonym under which the works of an author are entered is not his real name) has been dropped.

In contrast to this, the 1908 code (rule 38) recommended entry under the author's real name, and under pseudonym only when the real name was not known; similarly, the ALA code (rule 30) preferred entry under real name, though permitting entry under pseudonym:

(i) when 'the real name is unknown, or the author wishes it withheld';

(ii) when 'the pseudonym has become fixed in literary history'; or

(iii) when 'two or more authors have written together under one pseudonym, to avoid a cumbersome heading'.

The British Museum's rule (rule 20) favours entry under pseudonym: 'Where an author, while concealing his identity, writes under a descriptive or fictitious name, it is taken as a Heading if it takes the form of a real name . . . Names known to be fictitious are followed by the abbreviation *pseud.*, and the author's real name, if possible, is added within brackets, *eg* Loti (Pierre) *pseud.* [*ie* Louis Marie Julien Viaud]. In the case of an author who has written exclusively or almost exclusively under one pseudonym (*eg* " Mark Twain ", " George Eliot "), all editions of works originally published under the pseudonym are entered under it, even though the author's real name occurs in the book.'

It will be seen that, curiously, the oldest code—the British Museum code, and the newest code—the 1967 Anglo-American code, more or less coincide in their ruling; and it is not difficult to appreciate the sense of this. It is really no help to any user to enter George Orwell under Blair, or Mark Twain under Clemens. In all cases, however, the cataloguer must make references from the name or names he has not used to that chosen for the heading.

For anonymous works, the 1967 Anglo-American code (rule 2) decrees 'Enter under title . . . a work that is of unknown or uncertain authorship'; but, 'If reference sources indicate that a certain person is the probable author of such a work, however, enter it under that person and make an added entry under the title'. This is in line with the recommendations of the 1908 code (rules 112-118), which favoured entry 'under the name of the author when known, otherwise under the first word of the title not an article', with added entries 'for titles of all anonymous works whose authors are known'; and of the 1949 code (rule 32), which stated, 'Enter works published anonymously under author when known', but, 'If the author is not known, enter under title'. The British Museum's complicated rule (rule 18) is on a different principle altogether. Anonymous works

(a) 'concerning a person (real or fictitious) named or adequately described in the title, are catalogued under his name';

(b) 'concerning a collective body or institution, named or adequately described in the title, are catalogued under the Heading proper to such body or institution';

(c) 'concerning a place, or an object bearing a proper name (*eg* a ship), named or adequately described in the title, are entered under the Heading proper to such a place or object.'

If none of these apply to the work in question—that is, if it does not concern, *and* name in its title, a person, institution, place or object—then the heading used is

(d) 'the name of a person or place (in that order of precedence) forming a necessary part of the title . . . or an adjective derived from the name of a person or place, when used as a noun, or as a compound expression containing such an adjective.'

The example quoted here in the British Museum *Rules* is that an anonymous work with the title, *A letter to Sir Robert Peel on the education of the middle classes,* is entered under the heading PEEL (*Right Hon Sir* Robert) 2nd Bart; that is, though the work does not *concern* Sir Robert Peel, his name 'forms a necessary part' of its title. If the title of the anonymous work contains the

116

name neither of a person nor of a place, the heading adopted is

(e) ' the first noun in the title '.

Thus, as the *Rules* instance, an anonymous work with the title, *A first book of algebra,* is entered under BOOK. This does not seem very helpful, for though, true enough, *book* is the first noun, it is the noun *algebra* which is the more memorable and identifying. Finally, when the title of an anonymous work contains neither name nor noun, the heading used is

(f) ' the first word other than an article '.

The *Rules* add that when the author of an anonymous work can be ascertained, this should be mentioned at the end of the entry. There is no question of entry under the author's name, except in the case of ' recognized classics ' such as *Hamlet* or *Divina commedia,* where the authorship, though not stated in the work itself, is ' a matter of common knowledge '. ' Such cases, however,' the rule concludes, ' are exceptional.'

It is generally accepted that entry under author is the basis of our catalogues. Consequently, even in the case of anonymous works, if authorship can be ascertained, then entry should be under the author's name. Thus the practice advised by the Anglo-American and the 1908 and 1949 codes is the one to be followed: where possible, enter an anonymous work under its author, but to guarantee ' ready access ' to the main entry, make an added entry under the title also. In this context of establishing the authorship of an anonymous work, the value of Halkett and Laing's *Dictionary of anonymous and pseudonymous English literature* (described in chapter III) should not be forgotten.

The rules for dealing with pseudonymous and anonymous works are the most important in the field of literature in English. The other pertinent rules—for commentaries, concordances, and manuscripts—are less vital.

For commentaries, the 1967 Anglo-American code's rule exemplifies one of the main respects in which the new code differs from earlier ones: the acceptance of title-page statements at their face value unless there is good reason to question the accuracy of their description of the work to be catalogued. Rule 11, in outline, runs as follows:

'A. *Commentary emphasized*. If the title page presents the publication as a commentary on the work, catalogue it as such . . . unless there is strong reason to catalogue it as an edition of the work. Such strong reason might be: (1) the prefatory material indicates that the primary purpose of the publication is to provide an edition of the work; (2) the text of the work is decidedly more extensive than the commentary; or (3) the commentary is typographically subordinate . . . Make an added entry under the author and title of the text.

' B. *Edition of the work emphasized.* If the title page presents the publication as an edition of the work with accompanying commentary or annotations, catalogue it as an edition of the work . . ., making an added entry under the commentator, unless there is strong reason to catalogue it as a commentary.'

To the three strong reasons paralleling those listed under A there is added a fourth: ' the text of the work is so broken up by the commentary that it cannot be read conveniently by itself '.

' C. *Title page ambiguous.* If the title page is ambiguous as to the aspect under which the publication is presented, catalogue it in accordance with the aspect emphasized by the prefatory material, by the relative extent of the text and the commentary, or by the typographical presentation of the text and commentary. In case of doubt, catalogue . . . as an edition of the work and make an added entry under the author of the commentary.'

Concordances are among the many different types of ' related works' covered by an extremely comprehensive rule of the new code (rule 19). In general, this rule will result in the entry of a concordance ' under its own author and/or title ', with ' an added entry under the author and title or under the title of the work ' concordanced, as appropriate. A concordance will only be entered under the ' author and/or title ' of the work concordanced if (a) it ' has a title that is indistinctive and dependent on the title of ' this work, *and* (b) its use ' is dependent on one particular edition of the main work '. A footnote points out that a ' concordance to poetical works that uses references to line numbers is usually applicable to various editions even though the particular edition used in its compilation may be named '. The merit of this rule is that it enters the concordance under its own author, and at the same time provides, *as part of the author catalogue,* an added entry under the

118

author and title of the work concordanced (or under its title alone, if it is a work so entered), thus reconciling the conflicting requirements of British libraries (with their emphasis on the author or name catalogue) and American libraries (with their emphasis on dictionary catalogues) in a common rule.

Finally, in this review of cataloguing rules pertinent to a collection of literature in English, it should be noted that the new code devotes a whole chapter (chapter 10) to the cataloguing of manuscripts, and that this chapter includes rules for description as well as those for choice of heading. The latter, as in the 1908 code and in the 1949 code, follow the rules for printed books as far as they apply: thus the manuscripts of an author are entered under that author's name.

All the foregoing has been concerned with the choice of headings for entries. The actual entries themselves present no peculiar problems in the field of literature in English. The only proviso here is that it is important, in the case of collections and anthologies, to make a feature of including contents notes in the entries for these. In many instances a library's only text of, for example, a particular play, might be that contained in an anthology of plays. To offer a contents note, however, is only half of the operation; the other half must be to make an added entry for each of the items listed in the contents note. This is not always practicable when an anthology or collection is a very large one; but where the library's only text of an important item exists in such a collection, then it must be indicated by means of an added entry. Added entries present no problem if the library's catalogue is on a unit principle—that is, the main entry is reproduced as many times as is required, and making an added entry only means adding another heading to a duplicate of the main card or slip.

General guidance as to the arrangement of entries is to be found in the *ALA rules for filing catalog cards* (Chicago, 1942). A particular problem which often arises in the catalogue of a collection of literature in English is how to arrange the entries under a voluminous author.

The *ALA rules* recommend that entries for such authors be arranged in the following main groups:

1) Complete, or nearly complete, works

2) Selected works, and selections
3) Single works
4) Works about the author.

The entries in the first group, complete works, are to be arranged by editor; or by series or publisher, if well-known; otherwise, by date. The second group, selected works and selections, are to be arranged by title. The third group, single works, by title. The fourth group, works about, by author of the work.

A more elaborate arrangement is suggested for large reference collections. Here there are seven main groups :
1) Complete works
2) Selected works : partial collections (miscellaneous)
3) Selected works : particular groups
4) Single works
5) Spurious and doubtful works
6) Selections : anthologies, extracts, quotations, etc
7) Subject entries.

Within group (1), Complete works, the arrangement is detailed :
a) Manuscripts and facsimiles of manuscripts, by date
b) Texts in the original language, first by date and then by editor
c) Translations, alphabetically by language, and within language by date
d) Criticisms of a particular edition or translation, to follow immediately after that edition or translation.

Group 2, Selected works : partial collections, are to be arranged like complete works. Group 3, Selected works : particular groups, are to be arranged by the best-known group-title. Group 4, Single works, are arranged by title, and the entries under each title are to be divided into a) Texts, b) Translations, and c) Criticism. Group 5, Spurious and doubtful works, are to be arranged into a) Collections, and b) Single titles. Group 6, Selections : anthologies, etc, are to be treated like group 1, Complete works.

The *ALA rules* also offer an alternative elaborate arrangement for large collections whereby ' translations and criticisms form separate groups following the entire body of original texts '. The main groups therefore become :
1) Original texts
2) Translations

120

3) Biography and general criticism

4) Criticism of individual works

5) Other subject entries.

The original texts are arranged into:

a) Complete works

b) Selected works

c) Single works

d) Spurious and doubtful works

e) Selections

It must not be thought that the *ALA rules for filing* are the only or final word on the subject of arranging the entries of a voluminous author. The British Museum catalogue, for example, deals with Dr Johnson as follows:

1) Works, by date

2) Poetical works, by date

3) Miscellaneous collections, by date

4) Letters, by date

5) Single works, alphabetically by title; under each title, by date

6) Selections, by date

7) Translations, prefaces, etc, arranged alphabetically by the author of the book translated or prefaced

8) Biography, alphabetically by biographer's name

9) Miscellaneous, alphabetically by author's name.

Being a book-form catalogue, and therefore having to be economical of space, the British Museum catalogue does not, of course, supply main entries in groups 7 to 9, but only *see* references. Since the librarian of a collection of literature in English is not likely nowadays to be presenting his catalogue in the form of a printed book, but on cards or slips, he must avoid using *see* references of this type. A *see* reference is an irritation to the catalogue user, who should be supplied immediately with the information he is seeking, not directed to another part of the catalogue for it.

The librarian is not obliged to follow either the *ALA rules* or the practice of the British Museum catalogue in arranging entries for voluminous authors. Certainly, the *ALA rules* offer a very sound basis for such arrangements; but the librarian should exercise his own judgment as to what is most acceptable in the context of his own library. There is, however, one unbreakable rule: whatever group-ing of entries is adopted, it should be prefaced by a card (or slip) summarizing the whole arrangement, and further, each division should be clearly signalled by an appropriately-headed guide-card.

CHAPTER XIII

Classification

THE MAIN DEBATE in the classification of a collection of literature in English is whether the primary division should be by form, or by period. The two best-known general schemes of classification, the Dewey Decimal Classification and the Library of Congress Classification, embody respectively these two different approaches.

In the Dewey Decimal Classification, of the main classes 000 to 900, class 800 is the Literature class. Within 800, 810 is American Literature, and 820 English Literature. 820 is divided by form, as follows:

821	English poetry
822	English drama
823	English fiction
824	English essays
825	English oratory
826	English letters
827	English satire and humour
828	English miscellany
829	Old English (Anglo-Saxon) literature.

In the Library of Congress Classification, of the main classes A to Z, class P is the Literature class. Within P, PR is English Literature, and PS American Literature. PR is divided by period, as follows:

PR 1-978	Literary history and criticism
PR 1101-1369	English literature—Collections
PR 1490-1799	Anglo-Saxon literature
PR 1804-2165	Anglo-Norman period, Early English, Middle English
PR 2199-2405	English renaissance (1500-1640)
PR 2411-3195	The drama
PR 3291-3784	17th and 18th centuries, 1640-1700
PR 3991-5990	19th century, 1770/1800-1890/1900
PR 6000-6049	1900-1960
PR 6050-6076	1961-.

The chief argument in favour of division by form is that it assembles a particular form for recreational reading. In a public library, for example, readers prefer to find poetry, or plays, brought together in one place. It is also argued that the development of a particular form is more readily traced by this arrangement.

However, the opposing view is that English literature is usually studied by period, not by form. Certainly, period division is simpler and more easily applied. Also, it is generally held that any author is more of his period than of his form. Ernest A Savage in his *Manual of book classification and display for public libraries* (London, Allen & Unwin, 1946) quotes Hegel in support of this view: 'Every work of art belongs to its time, its people, its environment'. He denies that 'form is paramount', and cites the obviously unsatisfactory treatment of Shakespeare in the Dewey Decimal Classification: his plays in 822, his poetry in 821, his biography in 928, his local associations in 914.248 (Warwickshire). He also points out other howlers which result: for example, John Donne in Satire and humour, not in Poetry. Savage's unfavourable examples are easily multiplied, for the single, simple reason that very few authors have confined themselves to only one form, and therefore, division of a collection of literature by form automatically necessitates either a series of awkward compromises in the treatment of particular authors (that is, for instance, classifying all a poet's work, whether in the form of poetry or not, in 821, because he was *primarily* a poet), or a totally unsatisfactory separation of their works.

The important thing in an English collection is to bring together the works of a particular author. Division by form cannot do this. Such is the negative argument in favour of division by period; and when the positive and practical arguments in favour of period division—that this is how the subject is studied, that period is more meaningful than form, that period division in application creates considerably fewer problems and anomalies—are also taken into consideration, then it becomes difficult to accept the Dewey Decimal Classification's approach to literature.

A secondary debate in the classification of literature in English is whether English language and English literature should be classified together. Both the Dewey Decimal Classification and the Library of Congress Classification separate English language from

English literature. Dewey devotes class 400 to Language, English being 420, divided as follows:

421 Writing
422 Derivation
423 Dictionaries
424 Synonyms, homonyms, antonyms
425 Grammar
427 Patois, slang, dialectology
428 Texts for learning English language
429 Old English (Anglo-Saxon), 500-1110 AD.

Library of Congress uses P for both Language and Literature, but while, as was noted earlier, English literature is at PR and American literature at PS, English language is separated from them, being allocated PE. A host of other languages and literatures occur between PE and PR—for example, PQ contains all the Romance literatures. PE is divided as follows:

PE 1-71   Philology
PE 101-299   Anglo-Saxon
PE 501-685   Middle English
PE 801-896   Early Modern English
PE 1001-1693   Modern English
PE 1700-3729   Dialects.

Keeping all the languages together—at 400 in Dewey and in the early part of P in Library of Congress—is of undoubted value in comparative language studies; and on the level of the very general library user, it means that all dictionaries and all grammars are grouped in one area. But balancing this, is the fact that a language and its literature are more commonly studied together than is one language with another language. There is the whole set of arguments which support the provision of English dictionaries in an English literature collection: in brief, that works on a language—not just dictionaries, but also grammars, and treatises on style, composition, rhetoric, prosody—are the keys to the literature written in that language. Even among the writers themselves obvious links are broken: Johnson the essayist is separated from Johnson the lexicographer.

On balance, it is usually conceded that English language and English literature are best classified together. But since neither

Dewey nor Library of Congress make provision for this, various makeshift arrangements are very often employed. In libraries using Dewey the method frequently adopted is to shelve class 400, Language, out of sequence, placing it next to 800, Literature. This is unsatisfactory on at least two scores. First, it is a negation of the notation. Notation, after all, is merely a means of coding an arrangement. Thus if that coding is 000 to 900, it is nonsense to offer this as 000, 100, 200, 300, 500, 600, 700, 400, 800, 900; what on earth are the poor users to make of it? Second, placing 400 adjacent to 800 is only placing Language next to Literature; not 420, English language, next to 810, American literature, and 820, English literature.

Library of Congress users have also been inventive. PE could be taken out of sequence, and placed next to PS and PR; but this fails on the same grounds as making 400 follow 700 and precede 800. However, one of the best notational tricks has been to make English language, instead of PE, become the amalgamation PRE, so that the sequence runs PR, PRE, PS, PT, etc. The same can be done for German, where PD is Language and PT is Literature. Thus the Language and Literature sequence then runs on the lines:

PR   English literature
PRE   English language
PS   American literature
PT   German literature
PTD   German language.

Again, though, it smacks of the makeshift, since the usual Library of Congress notation is a combination of two letters and four numerals. A sequence of notations incorporating first of all mysterious gaps, and then unfamiliar three-letter prefixes, is not too helpful.

So far, the Dewey Decimal Classification and the Library of Congress Classification have been surveyed in the light of the two main approaches to the arrangement of literature; and in the light of the desirability of placing together language and literature. A few more general comments on the two schemes may be offered.

On the whole, the Dewey system is more frequently found in public libraries, whereas the Library of Congress system tends to be favoured by academic libraries. This will be readily appreciated if the respective schedules are examined. Dewey has a shorter, more easily remembered, and more readily apprehended, notation. Its outlines are simple, its detail negligible: there are, for example, a few form divisions, such as .03 Dictionaries, .08 Collections, .09 History, which can be attached to the standard notations—for example, 821.08 is a collection of English poetry. And as was noted earlier, Dewey's primary division by form does group Poetry, Plays, and the rest, in a way which suits the needs of a general, and principally recreational, library. Library of Congress, on the other hand, is exhaustive in its detailed enumeration, and the literature schedules have a bibliographic value in their own right. For each of the authors enumerated, a set of tables is supplied for the arrangement of works by and about them. These tables range from one containing 98 numbers (for major authors such as Wordsworth), down to one offering an arrangement for a minor author meriting only a Cutter number (Cutter numbers in Library of Congress are a device by which an author's surname is represented by one letter plus one or more numerals—for example, the name Moore could be represented as M6). The usual breakdown provided for an author in Library of Congress is:

Collected works
Translations
Selections
Separate works
Biography and criticism.

Where the scheme breaks down is in its allocation of notation for the twentieth century. Since only PR 6000 to PR 6049 is provided for the full alphabetical sequence of authors writing between 1900 and 1960, it means that Cutter numbers proliferate. Another flaw is that the basic period divisions are too long, and this produces odd alignments on the shelves, such as Shaw rubbing shoulders with Shelley. On the whole, though, Library of Congress is more to be preferred than Dewey.

The other general schemes available are surveyed in J Mills's *A modern outline of library classification* (London, Chapman & Hall, 1960), a useful and convenient guide which makes comparison of the treatment accorded to literature by the various schemes very easy. Of these schemes, J D Brown's *Subject classification* is valueless, since it separates literary history and criticism (M) from forms and texts (N); separates books on language from texts in that language; and offers under each literature the most inadequate period divisions. The *Universal decimal classification,* based on Dewey, is an improvement on the original. Mill writes: ' Class 8 is notable for being the most prominent example of a fully synthetic class in the UDC. The primary facet, Language, is the only one enumerated (82/89). The other three facets are obtained by Auxiliaries (Literary Forms -1/-9; Problems and techniques .01/.09; Periods " "). In the Problems facet, .07 is Philology, which allows the collocation of Language and Literature if desired (although in a rather unhelpful position).' However, despite the improvements, and despite Mills's enthusiasm for the faceted as opposed to the enumerative approach to classification, the Universal Decimal Classification is still sufficiently related to Dewey in its basic approach to make it a poor choice for the classification of a collection of literature in English. Bliss's *Bibliographic classification* is the only general scheme which keeps languages and literatures together; but as a scheme it is so permissive that, as Mills remarks, ' It is hardly an exaggeration to say that virtually any arrangement of literature (history and texts) which is desired may be achieved in the BC '. The very fact that there is ' generous provision for alternatives ' makes for difficulties in applying it consistently. Two features in its favour, again quoting Mills, are ' the very careful collocation of the major classes ' and ' the exceptionally brief notation '.

In the introductory chapter of this textbook it was remarked that once a suitable scheme for a collection of literature in English has been chosen, applying it is a very straightforward matter. This is in essence because the standard method of arrangement within the primary division by form or period is merely alphabetizing the authors represented. Thus the product of a literature classification, except in preliminary sections such as literary history, is basically a series of alphabetical sequences, classifying into which presents few problems.

One of these problems is how to deal with authors some of whose works, though of literary interest and value, are concerned with other subjects. The examples which spring to mind are Arnold (and education), Carlyle (history, of course), Ruskin (and art), T E

Lawrence (and Arabia), Shaw (and socialism). Classifying such authors is a matter of weighing the subject value of the work against the literary eminence of the writer. If the classifier decides that the interest of the work in hand to the library's users lies in its being part of English literature, he must still not neglect to make an added entry in the subject catalogue under the topic it concerns. Similarly, if the classifier decides to place the work with the subject it treats, he can reflect that the library's author catalogue will display it in conjunction with the writers' other purely literary works. A compromise solution often possible is to classify in literature the collected works of a writer of literary importance, but to place single or duplicate volumes of his with their particular subject.

Mention has just been made of the subject catalogue in a library. Literature is so much regarded as a form that it is very easily overlooked that, even so, in many of its aspects literature needs to be approached from a subject angle. Plainly, the author catalogue of a collection of literature is the vital one, and it would be wasteful to repeat its work by, for example, duplicating all fiction entries in a subject catalogue. However, apart from the individual literary creations of particular authors, there will be in an English collection general works on aesthetics, technique, literary criticism and literary history; works on particular forms, or collections of a particular form; works on particular topics (for example, allegory); and special categories of work, such as bibliographies or books of quotations. To all of these, a subject catalogue approach is both valid and necessary.

Subject catalogues can take two main forms. The first is the classified form: that is, entries are arranged in class-mark order, producing an order parallel to that on the shelves. For many years, in Britain, this has been the favoured form, since it is argued that, apart from the obvious administrative advantages of a parallel record, it also provides a finer-edged analysis of the subject content of books. What such arguments ignore is the fact that in paralleling the order on the shelves nothing extra is contributed in the way of assisting the user; and what is the clinching argument, most users seem chary of consulting a classified catalogue. The almost universal provision in this country, in such libraries as have a subject catalogue, of the classified form is a striking example of how assistance to readers has taken second place to administrative convenience. A classified catalogue, of course, needs an alphabetical index of subject terms if effective use is to be made of it; and the production of such an index is a sophisticated technique in its own right. The overall result of this combination of a classified sequence of entries with a complex index as its key, is a subject catalogue which might be justified theoretically but which actual use by readers does not support.

The alternative form to the classified is the alphabetical-subject catalogue. Here entries are grouped under alphabetically-arranged subject headings. The largest list of such headings is that supplied in the *Subject headings used in the dictionary catalogs of the Library of Congress*. The main advantage of the alphabetical-subject catalogue is that it is easily comprehended by and therefore attractive to library users. Hence its prevalence in the United States.

It is a particularly useful form for providing a subject catalogue to a collection of literature in English. First, the national literatures may be grouped. For example:

AMERICAN LITERATURE

ENGLISH LITERATURE

For these, period and other division is provided; for example:

ENGLISH LITERATURE—Addresses, essays, lectures

—Bibliography

—History and criticism

—18th century

—20th century

Each period division may be further subdivided:

ENGLISH LITERATURE—18th century—Collections

—18th century—History and criticism.

Second, headings are also provided for the various forms, both separately and as part of a national grouping. For example:

POETRY—Collections

—History and criticism

—Study and teaching

and

ENGLISH POETRY—Addresses, essays, lectures

—Dictionaries

130

—History and criticism

—Indexes.

Third, headings are provided for special topics. For example:

ALLEGORY

POETIC LICENCE

ROMANTICISM.

The Library of Congress *Subject headings* list is nearly 1,500 pages long, and quite exhaustive. More importantly, it also supplies the entire network of cross-references required by such a system.

CHAPTER XIV

Exploitation

IN GENERAL TERMS, what has been said in the last two chapters concerns exploitation. If a librarian provides an author catalogue with liberal added entries, an alphabetical-subject catalogue equally liberal in added entries (for though a book can only occupy one place on a shelf, it may treat of many subjects, all of which should be represented under the various appropriate headings in the subject catalogue), and a successful classified arrangement on the shelves, then he is most certainly exploiting his collection. Besides these basic requirements, however, exploitation also includes the compilation of reading-lists for the library's users, the presentation of book-displays, specialization in one or more areas in the field, and co-operation with other libraries.

Reading-lists and book-lists are usual in all types of library. The commonest example is the list of recent additions. The majority of academic libraries issue one regularly; in addition, most academic libraries possess rare book collections from which they assemble frequent exhibitions, and compile book-lists or catalogues to accompany them. Public libraries, as well as lists of current accessions, take pride in producing attractive reading-lists to engage, encourage and assist their readers.

The recent additions lists issued by academic libraries rarely include annotations. They list each newly-acquired title in the form of a compacted version of the standard catalogue entry, and group them under broad subject headings. These lists are not normally selective; they itemize everything that has been received. Distributed both within the university and outside it, they constitute an essential source of information to the library's users. A complete contrast is afforded by the special exhibition catalogues which academic libraries also prepare. Such exhibitions take months to plan, assemble and set out. The catalogues accompanying them do not cover a great number of items, but since these items are prized by the university, great care, skill and knowledge are employed in providing lengthy annotations; for the same reason, these catalogues are very often handsomely produced.

The recent additions list of a public library is invariably selective. Its aim is to advertise its more interesting new acquisitions, frequently concentrating on only one section of the field: recent poetry, new books on the drama. A mere listing of these items is not considered sufficient. For each, an annotation is provided; such annotations aim to be concise, informative and interesting. Public libraries also prepare annotated reading-lists based on their standard book-stock, drawing attention to particular sections of it. Such reading-lists are issued in response to a current interest or need, or to mark an event or anniversary. Sometimes they are issued with the intention of actually creating interest in a neglected area of stock.

Very often a public library presents a book-display in conjunction with a reading-list. Book-displays are a public library's window-dressing, and it is impossible to over-state their value. Part of exploitation is to make a library a visually attractive place. Its users, after all, have become accustomed, in department stores and supermarkets, to very competitive standards of display and advertisement. A library cannot afford to be dowdy; it is not invading any intrinsic principle of librarianship to provide gaily-coloured walls, stylish furniture, smart shelving and book-displays of a professional standard. Amateurishness in book-displays has to be avoided. A crudely-stencilled card fixed above a half-filled book-trough is unpardonable. A large library should employ on its staff especially for displays somebody with a training in commercial art. If such a person cannot be afforded, the next best thing is to see that the assistant responsible for display work is adequately equipped with all the modern materials and tools necessary to achieve a high standard.

One neglected area which can benefit from the stimulus of a book display are the classics. As an educator, and as the custodian of an important heritage, the librarian of a public library has a duty to introduce, or reintroduce, his readers to the masterpieces of English literature. A first step, of course, is to provide on his shelves varied and attractive editions of these. Small-print editions in shabby condition, or in grim institutional bindings, disgrace any library, especially when *Oxford illustrated, Zodiac* and other modern issues are so readily available.

A broadcast or televised production of a classic, or its appearance in the form of a play or a film, is always an excellent opportunity for the librarian to present an appropriate book-display and a related reading-list. Using the particular classic as his centre, he can assemble the library's pertinent material—the various editions of the work available; biographical and critical studies; historical and social accounts of the author's period. Even without the fortuitous help of the entertainment media, a librarian can arouse interest in the classics by arranging on the library premises talks and informal discussions. Another peg on which to hang promotion of the classics, is to emphasize any local associations of the great writers: at some time in his career, no doubt, Dickens gave a public reading from his works in the town. One device not to be recommended is to isolate the classics from the rest of the stock and feature them as a separate group: perhaps with some added incentive such as allowing them to be borrowed on non-fiction tickets. A rather more positive approach is required: the line of attack should be that classics have been integrated with the westerns, the romances and the detective stories because they afford pleasure too.

Book-displays and reading-lists are very obvious forms of exploitation. Less obvious is subject specialization. A librarian has not completed his programme when he has set up an adequate overall coverage of literature in English. He must proceed to the next stage, which is to develop particular strengths in the collection. In many instances, where a librarian has inherited rather than founded a collection, he will already find that a particular form, or period, or author, or topic, has been well represented. Given such a start, it is usually wise to maintain and build on this. Occasionally, a librarian will find himself in the position of being able to indulge a personal interest. There is no danger in this, just so long as he is prepared to restrain his indulgence in accordance with the same set of factors which govern any other venture into subject specialization.

The first of these factors, of course, is that the librarian must be confident that his general collection is such that he can afford the special financial outlay. The second factor is that he must be sure that in his choice of speciality he is not competing wastefully with another library, especially with one in his own region. The other factors are variable: for instance, if a librarian has a choice of specialities, he could very well settle for that which might attract gifts locally; another instance would be that if the general collection in question was a very large one, and therefore any specialization would be on an important scale, the librarian would have to include in his assessments the extra demands on staff and library space.

One obvious responsibility in specialization is towards any famous local author. In fulfilling this responsibility the librarian is serving his community, posterity, literature and literary scholarship. If he does not accept the responsibility, there is little likelihood that anybody else will, and the material will steadily disappear. Again he must never duplicate wastefully the efforts of another institution or person; but having established the need and accepted the responsibility, he must purchase and solicit material assiduously; feature his special collection prominently, perhaps even devoting a particular room in his library to it; seek publicity by means of posters, leaflets and press notices; and produce catalogues and book-lists.

In exploiting his collection, a librarian must look beyond the walls of his own library. No librarian can provide every book his users require from his own stock; he must therefore participate in interlending schemes with other libraries. The interlending network between British libraries is highly-developed. The most recent account of this, along with other aspects of co-operation between libraries, is to be found in G Jefferson's *Library co-operation* (London, Deutsch, 1966). Jefferson describes the present 'two-tiered pattern' of interlending, the centre of which is the National Central Library: public libraries interlending through the regional bureaux, university and special libraries interlending direct.

The logical extension of co-operation between libraries in interlending, is co-operation in storage, acquisition, and specialization. An example of co-operation in storage is the scheme known as the Metropolitan Joint Fiction Reserve, which was begun in 1946, whereby the librarians of the twenty-eight Metropolitan Boroughs divided the alphabet between them and each maintained in their libraries a reserve pool of the works of fiction by the authors in their alphabetical section; and each undertook to receive and store discarded volumes appropriate to their section from the other libraries. An article by K G Hunt (*The Metropolitan Special Collections Scheme after ten years,* in the *Library Association record,* January 1959), reported that the Metropolitan Joint Fiction Reserve ' now amounts to 67,589 books '; and noted that the ' routine operation of the scheme produces without fuss a copy of an 1840 novel, forgotten by all but the student, or an out-of-print novel of the early '30s '. The library responsible for a particular alphabetical section may not discard a volume from that section until a replacement copy is found. The value of such a scheme in the preservation for posterity of works of fiction is consequently very considerable. It is also a perfect example of exploitation by means of co-operation between libraries: as a result of it, the users of all the libraries concerned have had a vast collection of fiction—a collection no one library could possibly provide and maintain on its own—made available to them.

An example of co-operation in acquisition is the Background Materials Scheme begun in 1949 by the Joint Standing Committee on Library Co-operation. The importance of older British books in the study of English does not need emphasizing, but until the Background Materials Scheme, no systematic attempt was made on a national basis to acquire and preserve them. The libraries in which older books are especially important are the large public libraries and the university libraries; and a Sub-committee, formed in 1951, of the Joint Standing Committee, arranged that a group of such libraries each undertook to buy material within a certain period (usually ten years) between 1510 and 1800. This period allocation was done as far as possible in accordance with existing collections and interests. Thus there was achieved a national, unwasteful coverage of pre-1800 books among the libraries dependent on them.

Finally, an example of co-operation in specialization is provided by the Metropolitan Special Collections Scheme, begun in 1948. Here the twenty eight Metropolitan Borough libraries divided the Dewey Decimal Classification into fifty five sections, and each accepted responsibility for purchase and retention of one or more of these sections. Again there was an attempt to match the allocations with existing collections and interests.

The intention behind all forms of library co-operation is to make available to all library users the entire bibliographical resources of the country; in other words, the aim of library co-operation is complete exploitation.

CHAPTER XV

Outstanding collections and important associations

IT WOULD BE most useful if there was a handbook to the outstanding special collections and important associations in the field of literature in English. Unfortunately, no such handbook exists, and the librarian is obliged to piece together this vital information from a small number of inadequate sources.

Special collections range in size from small local collections, such as the Mrs Gaskell collection in Manchester Public Libraries, to Wise's Ashley Library in the British Museum with its eleven-volume catalogue. Their value and importance lie in the fact that first, they contain materials not elsewhere available, and secondly, that these materials, along with related items, have been assembled conveniently in one place. Thus the scholar or student can collate manuscripts, editions and variants, and have access at the same time to a comprehensive, even exhaustive, reference collection of biographical, critical and background studies not to mention—particularly in the case of special collections devoted to one author—unique items such as unpublished diaries, letters and personal papers. In addition, there very often exists—as with the Ashley Library—a printed catalogue to the collection. The librarian or curator of such a collection will invariably have become something of an expert in its special field. He can therefore be expected to give considerable advice and assistance to its users; to deal with postal enquiries; and perhaps even to supply photographic reproductions of items in the collection.

One of the best examples of a special collection in this country is the Tennyson Research Centre at the City Library, Lincoln, which comprises some 700 books from the library of Dr George Clayton Tennyson, the poet's father; about 4,000 books from the poet's own library; a comprehensive collection of books and articles on Tennyson's life and works; an almost complete set of first and other important editions of the works themselves; a large number of proofs corrected in the poet's own hand; a collection of family papers, including important family diaries; household books and publishers' accounts; and a great number of letters from eminent Victorians. Facilities for study are provided, and staff are available to advise; there are also photocopy and photographic services at special rates for research purposes. The Tennyson Exhibition Room at the Usher Gallery, Lincoln, contains manuscripts, letters, portraits and personalia; and an annotated, illustrated catalogue relating to this can be obtained from the City Library. There are even tape recordings of original phonograph records of the poet reading from his works, available for loan for special purposes.

The standard guide to special collections in Britain is the *Aslib directory* (London, 3rd ed, 2 vols, 1968-70), edited by Brian J Wilson. Literature is dealt with in vol 2 of this work: *Information sources in medicine, the social sciences and the humanities.* The major part of this volume—the first 644 pages, in fact—is a listing of libraries, societies and other organizations. For each, following its name, is given address, telephone number, title of official to whom enquiries are to be addressed, subject scope, and details of bookstock. The entries are arranged geographically, being grouped under postal towns; the postal towns themselves are arranged in strict alphabetical order. Within postal town, the entries are arranged alphabetically by the first word of the title. The volume also contains details of national, regional and local schemes of library cooperation, arranged alphabetically by name of scheme; and an overall index of the names of the institutions covered by the volume.

However, the key feature of the work is its alphabetically-arranged subject index. To locate outstanding collections in his field, all the librarian of an English literature collection needs to do is look under such headings as English language, English literature, English drama, English poetry, English fiction, English dialects, English dictionaries, and so on, and he will find the entry numbers of appropriate libraries. Thus under English language, he will find 27 special collections listed, from that at Bath to that at York. Quite apart from such general headings, individual authors are also indexed; thus under William Cowper will be found the entry number of the collection at Olney, and under D H Lawrence, the entry numbers for Ilkeston and Nottingham.

Such a guide can never be exhaustive; and because it is based on replies to questionnaires, it must be to a large extent unselective and uncritical. Nevertheless, it does meet a basic need in answering the question as to whether there exists in Britain a special collection devoted to a particular author or topic, and if there is, where it is located, supplying in addition brief information regarding the extent of the collection.

Further help with tracing special collections in London only may be obtained from Raymond Irwin and Ronald Staveley's *The libraries of London* (London, Library Association, 2nd ed, 1961); the older, but still valuable, *The students' guide to the libraries of London,* by R A Rye (London, London UP, 3rd ed, 1927); and L M Harrod's *The libraries of Great London: a guide* (London, Bell, 1951). Other local guides include: *Library resources in Greater Manchester* (2nd ed by K Whittaker, London, Library Association/ Reference, Special and Information Section/North-Western Group, 1966); *Library resources in Yorkshire* (3rd ed by J. Bromley, London, Library Association/Reference, Special and Information Section/Yorkshire Group, 1968); *Directory of Northern library resources* (4th ed by G R Stephenson, Ashington, Northumberland County Technical College, 1967—for the Northern Circle of College Librarians); *Library resources in the West Midlands* (2nd ed by B G Staples, London, Library Association/Reference, Special and Information Section/West Midlands Group, 1963); *Library resources in the East Midlands* (ed by L F Craik, London, Library Association/Reference, Special and Information Section/North Midlands Group, 1969); *Library resources in South-West England and the Channel Islands* (ed by V A Woodman and J E Spink, London, Library Association/Reference, Special and Information Section/Western Group, 1965); and A N L Munby's *Cambridge college libraries: aids for research students* (Cambridge, Heffer, 2nd ed, 1963).

Special mention may be made here of the Arts Council Poetry Library in Piccadilly, London, a library of modern poetry in English open to the general public five days a week; books are available for reference and for borrowing. Also in London are to be found two

140

substantial collections of Commonwealth literature, one (described by its librarian in the *Library Association record* for January 1966) at the Commonwealth Institute Library, and another (and much larger) one at the Royal Commonwealth Society Library.

Tracking down special collections of literature in English in American and Canadian libraries has been made easy by the publication of Lee Ash and Denis Lorenz's *Subject collections: a guide to special book collections and subject emphases as reported by university, college, public, and special libraries in the United States and Canada* (New York, Bowker, 3rd ed, 1967). Libraries are listed under alphabetically-arranged subject headings: first alphabetically by state, then under state alphabetically by city, and then under city alphabetically by the name of the library. Thus if one looks under English drama, English fiction, English poetry, American drama, or similar headings, libraries holding a special collection in the field are cited, with brief notes. Collections devoted to particular authors appear under that author's name in the alphabetical-subject sequence.

Associations and societies in the field of English are related to special collections in the field in that they also represent an intensive concern with the subject, and aim likewise to promote and cultivate its study. Many associations and societies themselves maintain extensive special collections. In addition, such associations and societies may put out important publications; issue guides and book-lists; hold meetings; stage exhibitions; organize conferences; and arrange lectures. Section XIII of *Scientific and learned societies of Great Britain: a handbook compiled from official sources* (London, Allen & Unwin, 61st ed, 1964) deals with British associations and societies devoted to literature and the fine arts. This handbook used to be called the *Yearbook of scientific and learned societies;* after appearing continuously for nearly fifty years it was forced, by the advent of the second world war in 1939, to cease publication; it has now been revived by the British Council. The associations and societies described in section XIII are arranged alphabetically by name. Under each, there is a statement of the object of the society; details of membership; times of meetings; and a list of publications. Under the English Association, for example, its aims are stated as being ' To bring together those who are interested in

141

English Language and Literature, whether as writers, teachers, artists, actors or administrators; to act as a link between groups engaged in specialized work; to uphold the standards of English writing and speech; to contribute to English letters, scholarship, and research; and to spread as widely as possible the knowledge and enjoyment of English Literature '. The entry also notes that the English Association organizes lectures, conferences and social functions; and publishes the magazine *English, Essays and studies,* and *The year's work in English studies.* A contrast to the English Association in range of interest is supplied by the entry for the Kipling Society. Here the objects include: ' the issue of a quarterly magazine devoted to Kipling and his works, and research and commentary thereon; holding of discussions on Kipling's writings; the provision of a speaker on Kipling whenever asked for by any outside body, and the maintenance of a complete Kipling Library for the use of Members '. Details and descriptions of the type supplied for the English Association and the Kipling Society are provided for the majority of the important associations and societies in the field: such as the British Drama League, the Malone Society, the Modern Humanities Research Association, the Modern Language Association, the National Book League, PEN, the Philological Society, the Poetry Society, the Royal Society of Literature of the United Kingdom, the Society of Authors, and the Society for Theatre Research. The British Council does not mention itself in this section: but, of course, it is an outstanding example in that it promotes English language teaching and British studies; maintains British libraries abroad; stages exhibitions, shows and tours; and publishes *British book news* and *Writers and their work.*

Details of important associations and societies are also given in *The world of learning* (London, Europa, 1947-), which is arranged alphabetically by country. Under each country, there is a section devoted to learned societies, grouped according to their subject interest. Under Great Britain, for example, there is a ' Language and literature ' group of learned societies: the address of each society is given, along with its date of founding, a brief statement of its aims, its number of members, its officers, and a list of its publications.

INDEX

147

153

Wright, J, *Book of Australian verse,* 81
Wright, Joseph, *English dialect dictionary,* 69-70
Wright, L H, *American fiction,*
1774-1850, 43
1851-75, 43
1876-1900, 43
Writers' and artists' year book, 92
Writers and critics, 45
Writers and their work, 45

Wyld, H C, *Growth of English,* 74
Historical study of the mother tongue, 74
Short history of English, 74

Year's work in English studies, 47
Yeats, W B, *Oxford book of modern verse,* 80
Young, D, *Scottish verse, 1851-1951,* 81-82
Young, K, *Drama of the medieval church,* 53